Y0-BRG-638

CHOSEN

CHOSEN

A Holocaust Memoir

by

Eta Fuchs Berk

as told to

Gilbert Allardyce

GOOSE LANE

Published with the assistance of The Canada Council, Multiculturalism and Citizenship Canada, and the New Brunswick Department of Municipalities, Culture and Housing, 1992.

Back cover photo of Eta and Myer Berk at their home in Fredericton, New Brunswick, by Keith Minchin.
Book design by Brenda Steeves and Julie Scriver.
Printed in Canada by The Tribune Press.

10 9 8 7 6 5 4 3 2

Canadian Cataloguing in Publication Data

Berk, Eta Fuchs, 1923-
    Chosen
    ISBN 0-86492-131-4

1. Berk, Eta Fuchs, 1923- 2. Jews — Romania — Tasnad — Biography. 3. Holocaust, Jewish (1939-1945) — Romania — Tasnad — Personal narratives. I. Allardyce, Gilbert. II. Title.

DS135.R73B57 1992   940.53'18'092   C92-098693-5

Goose Lane Editions
469 King Street
Fredericton, New Brunswick
Canada E3B 1E5

I dedicate my book to the twelve members of my immediate family who perished together with the six million Jewish victims of the Holocaust. In recalling in these pages the happy and sad memories of my life, I was blessed with the love and support of my husband Myer and our children, Sybil and Joel.

Eta Fuchs Berk
Fredericton, 1992

Contents

Foreword

Eta Fuchs Berk is a Holocaust survivor living in Fredericton, New Brunswick. Hers is the extraordinary life of a Jewish woman who came through the Auschwitz death camp. She is one of those who knows "what it was like." She wore the yellow star, she lived in a ghetto, she rode the death trains, she lost her family to the gas chambers, she was a slave labourer, a displaced person, a stateless immigrant. Someone observed that such Holocaust survivors can be separated into two types: those who cannot bear to speak of it, and those who feel compelled to do so. For a long time, Eta Berk could not speak of it; now, in this book, she wants to tell the whole story.

What made her change her mind was the continuing lie of Holocaust denial. She wants to defend the memory of her lost loved ones against those in Canada who denounce the truth about the Nazi mass murder of Jews as merely "the Hollywood version of the Holocaust." No doubt they will not hear her. The lie they tell is deaf, truth-defying, and as old as the Holocaust itself. From the start, the Nazis themselves denied the Holocaust by trying to

cover it up in a secret language about "resettlement"; later, facing defeat in the war, they
attempted to conceal the evidence by destroying
the gas chambers and tearing up the rail lines
to the death camps. After the peace, surviving
Nazi leaders at the Nuremberg trials, in denying the killing operations, passed on the lie to
the next generation. Now it is told in Canada.

So the lie is becoming a legacy. And probably it will never end. Holocaust denial will take
a place with all the other lies about the Jewish
people that have been told throughout the
ages. This is because the real issue in Holocaust denial is not about history; it is about
psychology, about the make-up of certain personalities who appear to need Jews to hate and
who see life in terms of Jewish plots and conspiracies. Therefore no amount of evidence for
the truth of the Holocaust is likely to change
the minds of those who preach this "great
denial." Nor will our laws against hate propaganda stop them from trying to spread the lie
across the country. "It was worth it," said Ernst
Zundel at the end of his long and costly trial in
Toronto for spreading false news about the
Holocaust. "I got a million dollars worth of
publicity for my cause."

Against such true believers, the best defense
of a democratic society is educated citizens,
good schools, and an awareness of history. If

the truth of the Holocaust can bring out the worst in the personalities of those who deny it, it can bring out the best in most others. The way we respond to such dark and awful tragedies, the way we react inside, sometimes tells us about the make-up of our own character. A philosopher put it this way: "Remember, when you look into the abyss, the abyss also looks into you." The idea that the study of a great inhumanity to others will bring out the sense of humanity in ourselves is the hope of Holocaust education. For this reason, Eta Berk wants to speak in particular to young generations who want and need to listen and learn. "Older people have always taught the young about the world through stories," she says in the end. "I hope that my Holocaust story will help them to know and remember more about the experience of the European Jews of my time."

Every person of good will, however, regardless of generation, will be moved by these Holocaust memories. I learned about the life of Eta Berk during many long and sometimes emotional conversations with her around the dining-room table in her home in Fredericton. In this book, I have told her story in my own words, following her experiences step by step, just as she described them to me. Further, I have tried to place her memories in the context of the times, combining history and testimony, and providing background to her journey from the old Jewish world in Europe to a new life in Canada. The story is hers, but in many ways it is a story filled with experiences common to the Jewish people of Europe in the time of fascism and the Holocaust. "In our century," someone remarked, "real events have far surpassed the wildest imagination of novelists." Such is the truth in the lives of Eta Berk and her people.

Thus, to know our century, we need to know the story of these lives. Most of the six million Jewish victims of the Holocaust died in silence, taking their memories with them into death. So much more valuable, therefore, is the testimony of those who survived. Novelists, historians, film producers, poets, all have tried to tell the Holocaust story in their own way. But the story is most compelling when the survivors tell it themselves. Jewish memory, of course, has always been preserved in old books, passing from generation to generation, and sustaining the identity of this ancient people by connecting them to a common history. Now, in our time, the Book of the Holocaust, so to speak, is being added. It is made up of a lot of little books like this one, slender volumes by witnesses who, in a vast slaughter of innocents, somehow missed their turn to die. And were never the same again. Most of those still giving testimony are now old and near the end of their time. Soon their dialogue with us will end, the Book of the Holocaust will close, and nothing further will be added. Then the Holocaust will become "just" history, and we will be on our own against those who say that the whole thing never happened.

The Eta Berk story, therefore, is part of a larger literature of survival which concerns not only the Jewish people, but Jews and gentiles together. In this common history of the two peoples, each had a different role in the Holocaust: the victims were Jews, the murderers were gentiles — although certainly there were also large numbers of gentile victims of the Nazi killing machine. This book is a study in this history of Jewish victimization. Here, in the experiences of Eta Berk and her husband, whose life she narrates for us as well, her readers will see a Holocaust with two faces, one cold and passionless, the other fierce and barbaric. The Holocaust that Eta Berk witnessed in Hungary can be described as murder by bureaucracy, a routine in which Jews were "processed" for destruction by state officials and policemen, ending at Auschwitz where her family, together with the whole Jewish community of her youth, was killed out of sight and sound in the gas chambers. When, after the war, she married Myer Berkowitz, a Holocaust survivor from one of the Jewish *shtetl* towns in

eastern Poland, she came together with someone who lost his own family and community to
more primitive methods of extermination. He
saw a Holocaust red in tooth and claw, a barely
concealed slaughter in which Nazi murder
squads, face to face with their victims, shot Jews
in batches and dumped them into mass graves.
Here readers will truly look into the abyss.

But there is more in this book than the ways
of death in the Final Solution. Beyond her
description of events leading to all this mad
destruction, Eta Berk reflects in the end on
where the Holocaust had led Canada. Certainly
our country is very far from Auschwitz and the
killing fields of eastern Europe, but Canadians,
she notes, are involved in courtroom trials and
political debates about Holocaust denial, war
criminals living in our society, and ethnic quarrels carried over from the Nazi years in the old
world. Holocaust history is our history too.

This, however, is not a book of history, ob-
jective, detached, and footnoted. It is a book of
memories, in which some things from the past
remain vivid and passionate, and others are
dim and nearly forgotten. These memories
come out of the mind of a survivor who was
hungry and exhausted in Nazi hands, who was
numb, bewildered, and deceived through her
worst days at Auschwitz. Now, nearly fifty years
later, her memories are clouded further by

time and age. Still, we come closest to what is inhuman in the Holocaust when it is described to us in the human voice of one of its victims. And though the memory is weak, the will to remember is strong. If the lie of Holocaust denial will not die, neither will the truth of Holocaust testimony. "I survived the Holocaust," says Eta Berk. "Now I want the memory of the Holocaust to survive me."

Gilbert Allardyce

My Father's House

- one -

There is an old curse which says, "May you live in interesting times." For Jews, no times could be more interesting, more cursed, than the years of my coming of age in the period of the Holocaust. Like most Jewish girls from Hasidic families in the Old World, I received little schooling in my youth. But I soon learned the ways of the world well enough. I learned from the Nazis: I learned at Auschwitz, in a German slave labour factory, and at a camp for war refugees at Bergen-Belsen. One could say that I had a European education.

So I know about Auschwitz. I am one of the many who went into this valley of death and one of the few who came back out again. This makes me a "bearer of secrets," a survivor who saw the truth of the Holocaust with her own eyes, a living witness to what has been described as the worst crime in the history of humankind. Some 30,000 Holocaust survivors came to Canada after the Second World War. Since then, time has dimmed our memories and death in old age has reduced our numbers. Soon we will be gone. When we were in the ghettos and camps, we had a common fear that the world would never know what was happening to us. Today I fear that, after our passing, the world may not remember. Probably the Holocaust story will need to be told and told again to every generation. I want to tell you my part of this story. In particular, I want to tell it in opposition to those in my province of New Brunswick who deny the truth of what I am writing here. I want to defend the memory of loved ones who died in the gas chambers, and to bear witness to the reality of Jewish suffering in the Holocaust.

I was twenty-one when I arrived with my family at the railway ramp at Auschwitz in May, 1944. On that spot, since 1942, Jewish families by the hundreds of thousands had been lined up, "selected," and separated forever, some members going one way and some the other. My family went together to the crematoria; alone, I was "selected" to live. Sometimes the thought of this fills me with guilt; sometimes it makes me feel that there is something I still must do with my existence. Ever since, in any case, I have wondered why I was chosen to live. "Chosen-ness" is an ancient concept in Jewish tradition; it involves not only the idea that our people were chosen by God for a special role in history, but also that particular individuals are chosen to play a special role of their own. Our rabbis tell us that being chosen in this way does not mean privilege or superiority; instead it means that something more is expected of us, that we carry a special burden. At Auschwitz, I was of prime age to witness and remember — a young adult, mature enough to know what was happening, yet still young enough to carry the experience to generations many years into the future. Now I like to think that I was chosen to carry this burden of Jewish memory, to try to make the Holocaust experience part of the collective memory of all people.

Many survivors have already told their stories. Some describe how the Holocaust began, the first crossing into the unknown; my story is about the ending, the last months, when the Nazis had mass murder down to a science, and when almost everything about the Final Solution was already said and done. The meaning of most stories becomes clear in the final chapter. The final chapter of the Holocaust was about us, the Jews of Hungary. British Prime Minister Winston Churchill described the swift and ruthless destruction of Hungarian Jews in 1944 as "probably the greatest and most horrible crime ever committed in the history of the world." We were delivered to Auschwitz in the last year of the Second World War, at a time when Nazi defeat was certain, when liberation by the Soviet Armies was only six months away. By this time, the Allied governments were long aware of Hitler's plan to exterminate European Jewry; the neutral nations knew; the International Red Cross knew; the Papacy knew, churches knew, world Jewish leaders knew. If any tragedy in history could have been prevented, it was this one. Instead, the world allowed the Nazis one last slaughter. They made the most of it.

Remember as you read my story to think of two things. First, that these events should never have happened. And second, that they did happen, just in the way that I am now going to describe them to you.

The Nazis at Auschwitz were expecting us. I have read that in the weeks before the death trains rolled into the camp from Hungary, German SS units streamlined the machinery of destruction, reinforcing the crematoria chimneys, relining the furnaces, and laying a new rail spur leading straight to the ovens. This was the Holocaust at its most terrible and most efficient. The trains carried nearly 440,000 Hungarian Jews into Auschwitz between May and June, 1944. Few of us came out again. Lost were almost all the Jews of my little town of Tasnad in Transylvania. With them went everyone in my family who made the journey with me: my mother, my sisters, my sister-in-law, my little niece, just three years old. For me, the world of my childhood, the world of Jewish life in Hun- gary, ended with them in the fire and smoke of the crematoria. To begin my story, I want to go back and describe this world to you, to tell you what it was like to be Jewish in the centre of Europe in the time before the Holocaust.

This world before Auschwitz probably appears more bright and beautiful in my mind today than it was in real life in the period of my youth between the two world wars. Storybooks tell of Transylvania as the land of Count Dracula, dark in shadows and horror. To me, it was all happiness and sunshine, a place without ghettos, where Jews lived at peace, side by side with gentile neighbours. According to tradition, small numbers of Jews had lived in Transylvania since Roman times nearly two thousand years ago. In modern history, a new migration of Sephardic Jews, including my ancestors, came from Spain after Ferdinand and Isabella expelled them from that country in 1492. Later, numbers of Ashkenazi Jews, Jews of Germanic background, moved down from Poland in flight from Cossack massacres in that land in 1648. Over time, these migrants settled together in towns throughout Transylvania, where their numbers grew and prospered, and where their offspring in the nineteenth century developed close, patriotic loyalties to Hungary. Few of them, it seems, found interest in the rise of Zionism or the lure of Palestine. We thought, when I was a girl, that we were at home in the towns and cities of Transylvania.

My own town was lovely. Tasnad was located in the so-called seven hills region of Szilagy county in northern Transylvania, in a magic landscape of rural beauty, rich in wines, fruit and grains. It was a community on a hill, shaded under chestnut and acacia trees, with quiet streets and sidewalks rising gently in ter-raced steps toward level heights at the centre of the town. Some things were new to life there in my early years. I remember, for example, the first radio in town and the first automobile (which one day ran over its poor owner as he was cranking it up to start). Mostly, however, I remember a place fixed in time, where exis-tence was as slow and steady as the oxen that ploughed the surrounding fields. Most things necessary to life were still made by hand, right from scratch, and according to the old ways. This was small-farm, small-town, back-country Europe, and everywhere there were orchards, vineyards, and little mills where townspeople came to grind their own wheat and corn. The whole setting was idyllic, and my dreams today are still filled with the sun and scenery of my pure and innocent Tasnad.

Truly, however, you can never go home again. The pure and innocent Tasnad that I have described here no longer exists. Its Jewish population, like all of the Jewish communities of northern Transylvania, vanished in the air over Auschwitz in 1944. Afterwards, a few survivors, trying to keep alive the memory of these lost communities, wrote little history books on their past. The history of the Jews of Tasnad was written by my own younger brother, Abraham (we call him Bumi), an historian and professor now living in Israel. Not much is left standing in Tasnad itself to recall this community of over 700 Jewish souls (13% of the total Tasnad population in 1944) that he describes: an abandoned yeshiva, once one of the most famous in the area; two old synagogues; and the tombstones of a Jewish graveyard.

It seems that the oldest tombstone in this graveyard dates to 1805, but my brother traced Jewish life in the town back into the middle eighteenth century. His book tells the whole story: the coming of the first rabbi in 1833, the building of the first synagogue in 1867, the continuing quarrels over whether Jewish life should hold to old traditions or change to the ways of the modern world. My family held to tradition. We were Hasidim, the people of a golden tradition leading back to the famous Rabbi Israel the Baal Shem Tov of eighteenth-century Poland, a magic figure who taught his followers a faith of joy and prayer, bringing together spiritual emotion and a strict adherence to ritual law. Today an Hasid can be recognized on the street by his traditional dress, his black coat and round hat, his beard and temple locks. The word Hasid means "a pious one." My father was an Hasid in every sense of this word.

Jacob Fuchs was tall, slim, with brown eyes and dark hair, a man soft-spoken and gentle, beloved by his children. The bourgeois son of a bourgeois family of Szlatina in old Slovakia, my father came to Tasnad in the years before the First World War and eventually made his way comfortably enough as a petty merchant in the wine business. But, like most religious Jewish men of the Old World, my father lived a life of study of the sacred books of Judaism. As a young man, he had been a brilliant student at yeshiva, the schools of learning where Jewish males take instruction in the Talmud. As an adult, he corresponded with learned rabbis, put his own pen to religious subjects (years later, Bumi discovered some of his writings in an old collection of papers in the library at the University of Jerusalem), and, in the custom of Jewish men, set aside several hours every day for the study of scripture.

Soon after coming to Tasnad, Jacob Fuchs helped to found a second synagogue in the community, built for followers of the Sephardic rite, a version of Judaism generally more strict than that of the so-called Ashkenazi synagogue nearby. My father served his turn as *Gabba*, the president of the synagogue, and, as I remember it, he was always an honoured man in the congregation. The commandments, followed letter by letter, filled his days and every corner of his home. We kept kosher. This meant mostly keeping the rules about the food that we were commanded in the Bible to eat or not to eat, but keeping kosher involved much more than just the things on our table. Keeping Jewish tradition meant keeping a way of life that brought religion and ceremony not only to our daily diet, but to all of living — to work, play, dress, study, hygiene, and to all social and human relationships. This tradition set our family apart from the normal life of gentiles. It made my own life different from that of other children, drawing me together with Jewish playmates and holding me apart from non-Jews. Tradition defined my existence, setting rules over almost everything I did from morning to night, not just on Sabbath days or holy days, but every day. There is an old expression which says that, as a result of all these commandments, it is hard to be a Jew. But, to me, this Jewish life was very beautiful. Today, particularly on religious holidays, I feel a kind of melancholy that comes from the memory of my happy childhood in the home of my father.

Tasnad, 1923-1944

When I think of him now, I think of him especially as he used to be on the Sabbath, when he sang to his children, and when a peace and calm came over him, and over our whole household, that I remember as wonderful and enchanting.

After his yeshiva days, my father married Chaye Szasze Nutovitz, daughter of a middle-class Jewish family of the city of Sighet. In their years together, she gave him five children. First came my lovely sister Raizel, followed by brother Moise, who grew up tall and thin to look so much like my father. Next came sister Leah, fair and light, the only blonde in the family; then came Liebe, with the same beauty in darker colours. I was the baby, born on April 15, 1923, and only a year and a half old when my mother died in childbirth. I never knew her. Her appearance I know only from old photographs lost long ago during our deportation to Auschwitz. One photo, in particular, remains vivid in my mind. Present is a beautiful woman, finely dressed, almost regal, and wearing around her neck a gold chain bearing a miniature timepiece. This jewellery probably was one of those delightful gifts from the hand of my father, who, as a yeshiva student, learned the craft of jewellery-making, and, in later years, often fashioned little pieces to charm his wife and children. My mother's death so early in my infancy made me a favoured child, a chosen one, whom everyone wanted to watch over. Even after my father married again, and little Bumi was born, I remained the pampered child of the family. In fact, I was even pampered by Bumi, who from the first seemed closer to me than anyone else in the family.

The coming of a new "mother" changed nothing in the sheltered world of my father's house. Civye Bodner was the daughter of the locally famed Rabbi Uziel of Beszterce, a *dyan*, a Jewish judge, a man honoured for his high learning. Second marriages like my father's were common in old Jewish life, particularly when a widow or widower was left with children to rear and support. Normally these pairings were arranged by a *shadkhen*, the famous "match-maker" of Jewish legend. This time, my father was "matched" with a wife who had a quality rare among Orthodox Jewish women: she was educated. By tradition, learning in Judaic life was proper to the male; females looked to the duties of home and family, so Orthodox Jewish women in our town virtually never went as far as high school. In contrast, my new mother was learned in the faith and history of our people, and I remember seeing her read the prayers in Hebrew to the women of our congregation, who used to gather in our living room on the day of Tisha-Bav, the occasion when Jews sorrow over the destruction of the Temple in ancient Jerusalem. To her new children, however, this learned lady was a Jewish mother in the most endearing sense of the term.

She raised me through infancy and adolescence with the same love that she gave to her own child. I believe that I can say with modesty that I grew up to be a girl of quite good looks. A photographer's portrait of me from the years before the Second World War reveals a pretty girl about to become a young woman, with eyes dark and sparkling and a smile full of the innocence of youth. At that time, my future seemed clear before me: I would do what other Jewish girls of Tasnad always had done — find a trade and find a husband. Most girls who left school early had to learn some kind of craft to support themselves, and I began to take up work at sewing. My trade, in particular, was fashioning ladies' lingerie, a specialty I learned during a brief period away from Tasnad as an apprentice to a seamstress in the city of Sighet.

I always delighted in little travels of this kind, and especially I loved to take summer journeys by train to visit relatives. For the most part, though, my life was spent close to home and was as sheltered as any could be. As a good Orthodox Jewish girl, I was forbidden to date or even to be alone with boys. Always, when

Myself as a teen-ager, a pretty girl
about to become a young woman.

Tasnad, 1923-1944

boys were around, so was my mother. Sometimes young Jewish men from the yeshiva in town would come by to borrow books from my father's library, and one in particular won my heart. I must confess that I came to love him, although I never breathed a word of this to him. I never even held his hand. The most romance we had was when we sat together on the porch on summer evenings — next to Mother. Anyway, the war ended everything. My young man was soon gone, never to return. At the same time, as I shall explain, events began to close in on us.

Perhaps these memories of my happy youth are part make-believe. Perhaps I am remembering only the best parts, covering up the little troubles that always come between parents and children, brothers and sisters. If so, it is because of what came afterward. To me, everyone in my family was so blameless, so innocent, so much a helpless victim, that I have a need within myself to protect the memory of each of them. Once, when I was still little, my new mother described to us a dream in which my natural mother appeared to her and offered for the Sabbath meal a large cooked fish on a silver tray, a sign in old Jewish folklore of thanks and blessings. The meaning of her dream was obvious to me: my own mother was thanking her for her love and care for us. I need to idealize in this way the ties that bound together my lost family. Ever since this time, I have been trying to find again the peace and calm that I knew in my family home.

I cannot believe that our plain and innocent life could offend anyone. True, our Jewish traditions kept us apart from the gentile population, but otherwise I wanted so much to become one of the many, to feel part of the people around me. As students of history know, northern Transylvania had long been caught up in a mad quarrel between Hungarians and Romanians, with each side having nearly equal numbers in the territory. The area had been part of greater Hungary until the Hungarians came out on the losing end of the First World War in 1918. Then, as punishment, the western allies granted the region to Romania, even though Hungarians slightly outnumbered Romanians there. So, as a result, I was raised to be a good Romanian. In Tasnad, Romanians took over all the public posts from mayor to postman, and at school our Romanian teacher tried to teach us to speak Romanian, love the Romanian motherland, and honour the Romanian flag. Curiously, as a result of these long-ago lessons in my early youth, I probably know more about the history of Romania than of any other nation, and I can still repeat little stories from memory about Romanian heroes and battles. One story was about Mircia the Great, father of the ancient Romanian nation. Once, upon returning home in defeat from the battlefield, Mircia was turned away by his own mother, who refused to open the door to her son until he went back to the battlefield and returned in victory. Country above family. Within myself, I have always felt a longing for these ties that attach a people to love of country. However, someone said that all Jews carry a "bag of history" on their backs, the weight of centuries of anti-Semitism, setting them apart in the eyes of other citizens as outsiders in the nation. For this reason, I sensed myself to be Romanian and not Romanian, part of the people and not part of the people. Anyway, the rise of fascism in the 1930s settled this matter once and for all.

One day a gang of Tasnad boys was taunting some Jewish men in the street. One was my father, just returning from synagogue with little Bumi, who was still a small child and very frightened by all the shouting and commotion. Suddenly one of the gang put his arm around my father. "You see this man," he told the others. "Don't you dare put a hand on him. He's the best Jew in Tasnad and the father of the nicest girls in town." Later, Bumi liked to tell this story, to boast how much our father was admired not only in the Jewish community but among gentiles as well, even the rowdy ones. Certainly this story tells a lot about my father and his "place" in the Tasnad of my early years. But it tells more about the old anti-Semitism there. One element in the population, the so-called Swabians, a people of German ethnic origins, was known for open anti-Jewish attitudes, but they themselves were a minority in the area and perceived as rather cramped and old fashioned. In the larger public, hostility to Jews was more covert and controlled. We understood that gentiles probably talked about us behind our backs, but open outbursts of Jew-baiting — such as the gang that roughed up my father — were rare, and usually the work of hooligans with too much to drink. Polite society did not approve. Such old-style anti-Semitism was familiar to us, and we accepted it as a fact of life. It was hurtful and humiliating, but it was tolerable; it was an anti-Semitism that Jews had learned to live with a long time ago.

Fascism changed this. With it, as everyone knows, came a state-supported anti-Semitism that was murderous and dead sober. Little Tasnad was too far off the beaten path to attract the "greenshirts" of the so-called Iron Guard, the Romanian version of fascist stormtroopers, but the news of this marauding gang of Jew haters was a warning that life in the 1930s was becoming more dangerous for us wherever fascism showed its face. I am happy that my father did not live to see it. He was the idol of my life, and I was desolated when he died from heart trouble in 1934. But I am happy that he did not see what happened to his wife and children. I am happy that he was one of those gentle Jews who lived in the old world of Jewish life before fascism and the Holocaust.

To me, this old world changed in 1940. In September of that year, after Germany's summer of early victories in the Second World War, Hungary took northern Transylvania from Romania as a reward from Hitler and Mussolini for supporting the fascist cause. Frequently caught in the middle of national rivalries between Romanians and Hungarians, the 165,000 Jews of northern Transylvania had long experienced the anti-Semitism of both peoples at first hand. But nothing in the past prepared us for the madness of the Hungarian strangers who now entered our lives. We knew that the Hungarians were there because of Hitler. We knew that they had been hard on the Jews in Hun-gary. We knew that they were now going to be hard on us. We expected the worst; we did not expect the Holocaust.

I remember the day that Hungary marched

into Tasnad with flags flying and bands playing. Hungarians in town were joyous; crowds threw flowers to the marching soldiers, girls kissed them, flirted, and cried in delight. That night, people danced in the street. I envied my Hungarian neighbours this celebration of their nation in the same way that previously I envied the Romanians, but I knew that these marching men meant that changes were coming. Far off, the world outside had been at war for a year; the sight of these uniforms, guns, and leather boots made me feel that the war had now come home to us. Wisely, all the old Romanian officials slipped out of town before the Hungarians arrived. We Jews had no place to go. Our lot was to try to endure — and to put up with whatever came our way. Early one day, for example, members of a military marching band simply moved into our living room, took it over for a few weeks, went in and out of our house as they pleased, and finally moved on without a word of explanation. From then on, we were at the mercy of strangers, and these strangers had little mercy.

Most frightening to me was the arrival of the so-called Gendarmerie, special Hungarian police in dark uniforms and strange hats sprouting long black feathers. Fierce and menacing, these sinister figures appeared to me like a vision from hell. Most bristling among them were the Swabians, who seemed assured at last that the day of the *Volksdeutsche* had come to Transylvania. At this time, things Nazi and German were in fashion among many Hungarians. Collaboration with Hitler had rewards for their nation, and they wanted to show him that they could be counted upon in the New Order. So, throughout northern Transylvania new anti-Semitic laws, modeled on German race laws and previously enacted in Hungary itself, made our existence more difficult. Their purpose was to separate and isolate Jews from other citizens. And they worked like a charm. Hungarians came together by casting the Jews apart. This process was not the result of laws alone; people did their part.

Mostly, the young of Tasnad had always formed friendships within their own ethnic community, so that Romanian and Hungarian children generally played among their own kind and in their own language. Similarly, my own girl friends were Jewish like myself, particularly because our religious traditions made it difficult for us to share in some of the activities of other youth. Mainly, I guess, most of us just felt comfortable with companions like ourselves. But, beyond this, there was an open friendliness among all youth in Tasnad. We talked together in the street, we kidded with each other, we played together in the schoolyard. But with the coming of the Hungarians in 1940, new lines were drawn between us. Relationships turned cold and faces hardened. I remember girls walking arm-in-arm with Hungarian soldiers and pretending not to know me when I passed them on the street. Boys took to uniforms, youth organizations, and military service. In particular, I remember the night when two rowdies, just back from a stay in Germany and all dressed up in Nazi uniforms, celebrated their return by throwing rocks through the windows of Jewish homes. And I remember when the "May branches" stopped coming. Secretly placing May branches, branches of new spring blossoms, at the doors of neighbourhood girls was a happy May Day tradition among the boys in our part of Europe. More than just a sign of spring, May branches were a sign of friendship and affection. When the boys stopped leaving them at our door, that was a sign as well.

Tasnad was leaving us to the authorities, and these authorities began by taking away our men. I cannot remember exactly when my brother Moise was called up for service in the notorious labour battalions. These units, made up of men classified by the Hungarian military as too "unreliable" to bear arms for the nation, were attached to regular army formations as a labour force for the construction of roads and fortifications. Labour servicemen were drafted from among all the minority populations of Hungary, but everyone knew that life in the Jewish units became a particular form of hell. Before being drafted, Moise lived in peace and quiet with his wife and children in the small village of Csog on the Tasnad outskirts. There, as rabbi, as kosher butcher, and as moyl (the ritual circumciser of male children), he was the centre of Jewish religious life. Now, after Hungary joined in the German invasion of the Soviet Union in June 1941, this good and gentle Hasid was bundled off to labour on the Ukraine front, where winters were hard and Jewish life was cheap. In the same period my brother Bumi, who had left home to attend yeshiva at Budapest, disappeared into the labour battalions of that city, not to be heard from again until the war was over. Thus the men of the family were gone. The women came together and waited.

Eventually, there were five of us. Earlier my sister Leah and her child, a girl five years old, had returned home to live with our mother and myself. Next came my sister Liebe, whose husband also had been called away with the labour battalions. With her came her little daughter, Sossy, a beautiful child just three years old, whose sweet face still haunts me. Soon after, Moise's wife and two children moved in from Csog to be closer to Tasnad. So a circle of victims was formed: five women and four children.

Did we know what was coming? We heard rumours about ghettos in Poland, about "resettlement in the east," and about massacres of Jews elsewhere. Such news was hard enough to believe by itself; nothing prepared us to believe in the possibility of some mad plan to exterminate the whole Jewish people. We knew the old anti-Semitism; the new version was simply beyond our experience. History books note that there was virtually no resistance to the Hungarian Holocaust, and they ask why the Jews did not act in their own defence. Quite simply, we thought that we would survive. I have learned from experience that there is a vast capacity for "avoidance" in the human character, for avoiding thoughts of catastrophe, for avoiding dire conclusions about where events are leading. Looking back, I see just how naive we were at the time, how deluded and deceived. To the end, we thought that somehow we would come through. Resistance was the last thing in the minds of the helpless women and children in my house. So we waited, sheep for the slaughter. But, for a long time, the slaughter did not come.

Historians of the Holocaust have noted that, after the mass slaughter of Polish Jews in 1942, we Jews of Hungary were the largest block of Jews to survive in Europe. Beginning in that year, the Nazis, it seems, called upon the Hungarian authorities again and again to deliver us for destruction; each time, the Hungarians found reasons to delay and delay. So, as we survived month after month, and as months became years, our illusion of safety was easier to believe in than were the rumours of "resettlement." In our case, death waited around until the last year of the war in 1944. The reasons for this long stay of destruction, of course, were unknown to us at this time. The politics of the Final Solution took place far above the heads of the victims. Today, I know that history books tell the story as follows.

As long as Hitler was sweeping his enemies before him, Hungarian leaders were enthusiastic to collaborate with Germany in order to gain a share in the victories of the Third Reich. Thus when Hitler stormed into the Soviet Union in June, 1941, the Hungarian army stormed in right after him. For this, they would pay. As events turned against Germany in the following years, the Hungarian leader, Admiral Miklos Horthy, tried to disengage Hungary from collaboration in German racial policies. Part of this process was Horthy's stalling tactic on the "Jewish question," his slippery sidestepping of repeated German demands to bring the Final Solution to Hungary. By the spring of 1944, with the Red Army closing in upon central Europe day by day, Hitler would wait no longer. On March 18, he faced down Old Man Horthy for "betraying" their common cause. The next day, German forces occupied Hungary, a puppet government was placed in power, and SS units arrived to direct the Hungarian police against the Jews. The Russians were coming — but the Nazis got there first. Within days, SS *Obersturmbannfuhrer* Adolf Eichmann, master of the black arts of the Final Solution, was in Budapest to get the trains rolling to Auschwitz.

Some say that fascists were good at getting the trains to run on time. I believe that no one could be better than Eichmann. Between May 15 and July 7, a period of some two months, about 440,000 Hungarian Jews, over half of the entire Jewish population of the country, were deported to Auschwitz. As I have remarked, writers still find this to be one of the great tragedies in Holocaust history: the hour was so late, the Russians so near, the end of the war so close. But not close enough. Still, so many secrets about the Holocaust were known by this time that the Nazis found it impossible to keep these events out of the news. Previously, the deportations of Jews elsewhere in Europe were part of a secret history; in contrast, this deportation in Hungary was virtually a public event that could be followed in the western press.

I can remember seeing German soldiers on a truck passing through Tasnad on the day of the Nazi occupation. That was all I saw of them. Hungarians did the dirty work of the following months. Historians say that the Nazis got more help in carrying out the Final Solution from officials and police in Hungary than in any other country. One of Eichmann's aides said, in fact, that the Hungarians acted like "the offspring of the Huns" during the whole process. He should know. As elsewhere in Europe, the end came step by step, but now, with time flying, the steps came faster and faster. I suppose that, in retrospect, these steps together can be recognized as part of a larger, planned process. But to us at the time, all was confusion. Each new act against us seemed arbitrary, out of the blue, disconnected from anything else, and each was utterly bewildering, crushing upon heart and soul. The mind went numb. The body followed orders.

On April 5, the government ordered us to wear the yellow star on our outer clothing. Forcing Jews to wear distinctive markings of some kind to separate them from the rest of the population was an old medievalism, a practice that had disappeared from enlightened

Europe with the coming of the modern world. The Nazis brought it back with a vengeance. I have read that the Jews in Nazi Europe reacted in two ways to the order to wear the yellow star. Some determined to wear it with pride as a sign of Jewish identity; others looked upon it as the mark of a social outcast. Within me, both of these feelings mixed together, but the over-all effect was a profound demoralization. I simply withdrew into my home, feeling too ashamed to show myself in public. This, I understand now, was the start of an emotional separation — a real estrangement — from Tasnad that remains with me to the present day. It was my way of protesting against the betrayal and indifference of everyone I had known all my life, against the fact that no one came to help me.

Why did no one help the Jews? This question continues to haunt every history of the Holocaust. I know, of course, that in some places good people did help. In Israel today, at the Holocaust memorial called *Yad Vashem*, trees are planted in the memory of every "righteous gentile" in Europe who saved Jews from the Nazi murderers. Sadly, there were no righteous gentiles in Tasnad. We Jews expected no help, of course, from the new Hungarian political bosses who came to Tasnad in 1940 to take over the town from the Romanians. These men were always strangers to us. Nor did we expect anything from certain cranky anti-Semites in the old population. One of these was a Protestant minister, an old, blind man, tall and severe, whose Jew-hatred was notorious. Indeed the joke around Tasnad was that nature had struck him blind so that he would not have to look upon a Jew. Others could see very well, but looked the other way.

The Catholic Bishop of Tasnad, a town heavily Catholic in population, was a man who had known my father and all my family for as long as I can remember. As a girl, I played in his yard and climbed the trees on his grounds. When our time came in 1944, he said nothing for us. Neither did the priest of the Russian Orthodox church in town, an old man who seemed to care only for the minority of Ukrainians in the population who made up his flock. So it was with everyone around us. As the authorities closed in, our neighbours drew apart. What happened to Tasnad? Why, after Jews had lived in the place for over two hundred years, did the people turn away from us in this way? Was the cause in some patriotic rage? Was it in the fever brought by fascism? Was it the flags, the uniforms, the war? A mean mood was loose. Whatever the cause, this mood marked the passing of the old anti-Semitism and the coming of more terrible persecution.

For weeks there were rumours of roundups and reports that Jews were to be transported to ghettos for their own safety. Along with the rumours ran several cover stories. One claimed that, with the Russian front advancing on Hungary day by day, the roundups were necessary to secure Transylvania as a war zone. Another explained that the Jews were needed for war production work in Germany. The first clear evidence that something was coming was a government order forbidding all Jews to leave their homes. Henceforth, to get groceries and water from the town well, we were allowed to go out for only a few hours a day, always under the eyes of a "guide," a gentile who would agree to walk along with us and be responsible for seeing that we returned promptly. Our guide was an innocent young man from our district who accepted the task as a favour to us, and I thanked him for his troubles with a secret gift of a piece of my jewellery — something strictly forbidden by authorities, who had their own plans for Jewish valuables. In reality, this young man, quite without knowing it, was part of the net in which we were caught. While the police waited to pull it in, our neighbours kept it tight around us.

So we waited each day for the thing that we knew was coming: the knock on the door.

It came on May 3. Outside was a Hungarian policeman, a man quite gentle really, and even a little embarrassed to be upsetting a household of women and children. But, like everyone else, he had his orders. Each of us was to be allowed to pack a small suitcase, with just enough clothes, bedding, and food for a short period. All valuables were to be declared immediately and delivered over to authorities. Here was the beginning of a great pillage. Jewish valuables had become the talk of the town. In the last weeks, some of us, still believing that we would survive and one day return to Tasnad, asked certain neighbours in secret to take some of our valuables for safekeeping. Frankly, this was as good as kissing them goodbye. But most valuables were simply looted by the authorities. Officials, police, and plain citizens alike took on a wolfish hunger for Jewish money and jewels. We were hounded, plundered, fleeced. And it never stopped. Every mile of the road, all the way to Auschwitz, everyone with whom we came in contact wanted the same thing: jewels, money, gold, silver. I lost or gave away everything I had. Everyone in my family was picked clean, even down to the tiny earrings that little Sossy was wearing.

When our suitcases were ready on the day of the roundup, I watched the policeman take the keys from my mother and lock the door to the home in which I had been born and raised. He did not return the keys. At that moment, my mother went over and, with tears in her eyes, kissed the *mezuzah* beside our door. To fulfill the Torah commandment to put the words of God "on the doorpost of thy house," Jewish families attach a *mezuzah*, a little container holding a Bible verse, at the entrance to their homes. According to our tradition, God would protect homes marked with a *mezuzah* in the same way that, in Ancient Egypt, He once protected the homes of the Hebrews there from His commandment that the first born sons of the land were to be slain. But this miracle of the Passover was not repeated in 1944. Our Jewish sages have pondered this absence of God during the Holocaust. Why did not the heavens darken when the police came to our door? Certainly, after this, my Jewish existence would never be the same, never be as safe and sheltered, as it was in my father's house. The golden life that I lived there was what being Jewish meant to me. Now the authorities made it plain that we could not live as Jews like this any more, not in Tasnad, not in Hungary. Jews were not wanted here. When the policeman sealed up our home, he sealed inside the most beautiful and innocent years of my life.

After this, he marched us to a school building just a short walk away where, eventually, the whole Jewish population of Tasnad was herded together for one last night in the town. The school, I guess, was used in this way as a temporary transit centre in order to give local officials one last chance to shake us down, to grab what was left of our valuables. So the seven hundred Jews of Tasnad were held over for delivery the next morning, give or take a few poor souls left behind. Stories flew, for example, about the suicides of the Neumanns and the Kandles, two Jewish families that had converted to Christianity some years earlier. Imre Neumann was a prosperous banker, and no doubt he and Laszlo Kandle, a landowner with wide holdings in the area, hoped that their religious conversion would secure a place for their families in the Tasnad elite. But in the New Order in Europe, not religion but race, genes, became the difference between Jews and non-Jews. So these new Christians could not escape their old Jewishness. Thus the Neumanns and the Kandles, who became friends over the years, were lost between two peoples. When the roundup came on May 3, police found the couples together, dead by their own hand in a collective act of suicide.

This left only one Jewish person in town still free. Olga Bouer was a Jewish women who had married into the Antal family, the cream of Hungarian society in Tasnad, owners of the largest department store in the area. Hers was the only mixed marriage in town between Jew and Christian, and no doubt she was spared from the roundup for just this reason. Sadly, her own family, her mother and sisters, made the journey to the ghetto with us the next morning, when all the Jews of Tasnad — save Olga Bouer — were marched together from the school to the train station about a mile away at the edge of town.

I remember that the day was clear and warm, and my sisters and I took turns carrying little Sossy in our arms as we walked in silence along deserted streets. The scene was wretched. No one was in sight. Stores were closed up. In windows, curtains were drawn, although at times I could see eyes peeking through at us as we walked past. This was the way that old Jewish life ended in Tasnad. From all accounts, the scene was the same almost everywhere in Europe during the Holocaust: Jews being led away while gentiles watched, saying nothing, staying out of sight.

Would I have changed places with Olga Bouer at that moment? Truthfully, I had come to the end of all feeling for Tasnad. I simply wanted no more of the place. Those who wanted it *judenrein*, cleansed of Jews, could have it. I would not go near it again. I felt that I would die if I ever set foot inside it. From the day of deportation, I was one of those Jews made homeless by the Holocaust. As I said earlier, I always wanted to share the sense of belonging to a common homeland, to feel part of a people. Not this people. On the road to the Tasnad train station on that May morning in 1944, I thought that I was seeing humanity at its lowest level. I did not know that the worst was yet to come.

In the Eye of the Holocaust

- *two* -

I am a survivor. By this I mean not simply that I came through the Holocaust and lived to tell the story. I mean that something inside me brought me through experiences that others could not endure. Make no mistake, life and death at Auschwitz were largely out of my hands. Surviving there from day to day was mostly a matter of pure chance and luck. I was lucky. But I was strong as well. I have described my youth at Tasnad. Life there was gentle and easy, and nothing in these tender years gave me the strength to get through the Holocaust. Rather, I believe that I was made strong by the Holocaust itself.

"How was I able to survive at Auschwitz?" another woman survivor once explained. "My principle was: I came first, second, and third. Then...came all the others." This lesson is simple enough. Those survived who took care of themselves; those who cared for others died along with them. The Italian Holocaust survivor Primo Levi commented before his death in 1987 on this same hard and self-centred will to survive that separated the "saved" from those good and gentle Jews who simply went under

Auschwitz, 1944

in the death camps. He appeared to be convinced that survivors and victims were two
different personality types — one was hard at
the centre, the other was made of milder stuff.
But I think that there was probably little difference in the beginning between me and those
in the death lines at Auschwitz. I had no more
inner toughness than others in my family. But
the Nazis taught me to be tough. In the eye of
the Holocaust, I saw my enemy in a different
way. At Tasnad, I was willing to live with the
anti-Semitism that was part of everyday existence in old Europe. I learned in 1944 that
there was no living with the new anti-Semitism.
My response was not to rage and rebel; my response was to survive.

Do you believe in dreams? I had a strange
dream one night in my last weeks at Tasnad.
My father appeared to me and told me that I
would soon be taken away to a distant place,
that there would be great danger there, but
that if I did exactly as I was told I would survive
the ordeal. I remembered his words and his message: to obey meant to survive. And I obeyed.
Some writers argue that the Nazis were able
to kill so many in the Final Solution because
the victims were compliant and did not resist.
I admit that I was compliant. I did not resist.
In this, I was heeding my father's words and
keeping faith in his promise that I would make

it through. The result was that, for me, compliance and pacifism became ways of survival, ways to hide in the crowd, to avoid provocation and turn away anger. For some at Auschwitz, compliance perhaps was a sign of giving up; for me, it was a means to keep going. Auschwitz was the world of death but behind the wire fences there were also separate worlds of the living. Some prisoners lived on but lost all hope; these, the walking dead of the camp, were for some reason called the "Muslims." Others, in contrast, became more determined over time not to go under with the rest. I was one of them. Like them, I had the will to survive. But this did not come all at once. As the trials grew harder in the weeks after the roundup at Tasnad, so did my determination to endure.

These trials began for me in the ghetto of Szilagysomlyo (Szilagy Centre). This was probably the worst of the Hungarian ghettos set up in haste in the spring of 1944 as temporary internment stations for holding and softening up the Jews of Transylvania before sending them off to Auschwitz. Located on the site of an old brickyard about one hour by train from Tasnad on a main rail line, this ghetto was the collection point for Szilagy county, and within days of the roundups on May 3, 4 and 5, over 7,000 Jews were crowded into a confined area around two wooden sheds. Large numbers of these prisoners, unable to find room inside the sheds, remained in the open air and tried to find cover under makeshift tents of blankets and clothing. My family found a place in the loft of one of the sheds, and there we made beds in the hay on the floor and strung up blankets as partitions between ourselves and other families crowded around in every available foot of space. And we waited. The time was late, however, and the Jews of Hungary could not be kept waiting too long. In Polish ghettos, Jews suffered through a long captivity of cruelty and starvation that began in the first months of the war in 1939 and continued for years. In Hungary, with the war rushing to a close, this ghetto process, the process of brutalizing and breaking a people, was more swift, lasting barely one month.

The historian of the Hungarian Holocaust, Randolph Braham, has told the story of the hellhole at Szilagy Centre in his book *Genocide and Retribution.* In command was "one of the most cruel ghetto commanders in Hungary," the police officer Laszlo Krasznai, "the scourge of the ghetto," a man notorious for his sadism and brutality. Carrying out his orders, a special branch of the Royal Hungarian Gendarmerie, the terrible men in black uniforms and strange hats with long feathers, established a reign of terror in the brickyard. More, they allowed homegrown fascists and anti-Semites from the local population to come into the ghetto to take out their frustrations on the Jewish population. Making things worse, sanitation deteriorated in the overcrowded conditions. Pure water from one well was reserved for guards, but the water from our well was soon contaminated and caused high rates of intestinal infection. Braham estimated that as many as eighty percent of the prisoners suffered some form of infection and diarrhea. So dismal, in fact, were conditions of health and diet that, when the transports from Szilagy Centre arrived at Auschwitz in the next month, large numbers of deportees looked so run down and debilitated that they had little chance to survive the "selections" by the SS at the railway ramp. According to Braham, "the Jews from this ghetto had the highest percentage of selections for gassing and thus for extermination."

At the time, I knew none of these statistics, nor even the name of the ghetto commander. But I remember the awful violence of the brickyard. Scenes that everyone now sees in pictures in history books took place before my eyes. Laughing guards cut off the beard of old Rabbi Brisk, master of our Ashkenazi synagogue and yeshiva at Tasnad. Sons and daughters were beaten under the eyes of their parents; old people were beaten under the eyes of their young. Women were taken off to be raped. The favourite ritual of the guards was to hang men from poles, suspended by their arms, which were twisted around and tied behind their backs. Meanwhile, every day, the same mad hunt continued to get the rest of our valuables — there must be more valuables! We had been plundered, looted, but still the old legend followed us: all Jews are rich, laden with gold and jewels. From our side there was no resistance; we were too overwhelmed. No people should ever be as helpless as we were at that moment — especially if they are Jews. Our guards had a mass of stunned and subdued Jews at their mercy, at their pleasure. And that is what I remember the most: the look of pleasure in their faces. Their expressions were all hard and mocking at the same time. My mother tried to shield me from the worst cruelties, but my eyes were open. At Tasnad, I got used to anti-Semitism; I knew it and lived with it all my life. I never saw it like this before.

Still, the task of these guards was not to kill Jews. Their purpose was to isolate us, to break our spirit, and to make us easy to handle on the death trains and in the "selection" process at Auschwitz. The first transports began on May 31 when, according to Braham, 3106 Jews, packed in cattle cars, left the ghetto for the three-to-four-day journey through Hungary and eastern Slovakia to the killing centre at Auschwitz in Poland. Another train of 3101 followed on June 3 and a final shipment of 1584 emptied the ghetto on June 6. On the side of the trains was a sign reading "German Worker Replacement," an attempt by the authorities to continue the cover story that the Jews were bound for work in the factories of the Reich. By this late date, however, most of the world knew better. Yet Braham observed that the public outcry in Hungary was "pitifully small," and that it took another month for the western nations to bring enough pressure on Admiral Horthy to convince him to call off any further deportations. Horthy's order on July 7 saved most of the Jews of Budapest, but it was too late for those of the provinces, too late for us.

Raoul Wallenberg came too late for us as well. Humanity rightly honours this "righteous gentile" of Sweden who, at risk to his own life, in one of the most heroic acts against the Holocaust, arrived in Budapest at just this time to try to save the Jews from destruction. The New Brunswick writer Joseph Sherman, in his book of poetry, *Shaping the Flame: Imagining Wallenberg*, describes a haunting scene out of his own imagination. He imagines two trains passing in the night somewhere in central

Europe on July 8, 1944. One, rolling south, carries Wallenberg on his mission to Budapest. Looking out of the window at the precise moment, Wallenberg sees the other train hurtling by, north-bound, carrying the last load of provincial Jews on their way to Auschwitz. The scene is imaginary, but the timing is about right. Wallenberg crossed into Hungary after the Jews of the countryside were gone. The "righteous gentile" was too late for this last great deportation of the Holocaust. In his book, Sherman imagines as well the words that Adolf Eichmann might have used to describe this final act of the Final Solution: "It went like a dream." One month earlier, on June 8, police reported that all of Northern Transylvania was *judenrein*, except for the small number of Jews left behind in mixed marriages. So, weeks before Horthy's order, weeks before Wallenberg's train, the Jews of Tasnad already were dead at Auschwitz.

I remember the train that carried us there. "They can be loaded like sardines, since the Germans require hardy people." Thus read the secret instructions to officials for crowding us into the cattle wagons. So we were loaded like sardines. Before sealing the doors, the guards left two buckets, one for water (which was soon empty), the other for a toilet. Then began the journey into the unknown. At the city of Kassa at the Slovakian border, our convoy passed into the hands of the SS, and men in German uniforms replaced our Hungarian guards. The Germans took up where the Hungarians left off, shouting orders at us at every stop to deliver over our valuables. Somewhere along the way, one poor Jewish prisoner, quite by accident, kicked over the toilet bucket. His was a tragic case. The man recently had made his way back to his wife and child at Tasnad from a labour battalion on the eastern front, only to be caught with them in the roundup and deportation. When our train stopped for a moment, he was confronted by a German guard demanding to know who knocked over the bucket. Standing helpless with his wife and child, the man confessed. Instantly the guard raised a gun and shot him dead. Everyone was struck dumb, staring straight ahead in shock and fear. The whole event was monstrous. It was the first cold-blooded killing to take place before my eyes, and even after witnessing all the corpses at Auschwitz, I still remember this first murder as the most terrifying. The German left the dead man where he fell, and, for the rest of the voyage, the stink of death in the cattle car mixed with the smell of excrement, sweat, and unwashed bodies.

Primo Levi said that most Holocaust stories begin with a train. The boxcars and cattle wagons bound for Auschwitz were places of fear and filth, causing shock and disorientation among the passengers and further reducing them to a confused and docile mass. Thus the death trains not only transported the victims to the killing centres but provided the final conditioning for their arrival. I have seen the German photographs of the arrival at Auschwitz in late May, 1944, of Jews from the Carpatho-Ruthenian region of Hungary. Their train could not have been more than a few weeks ahead of our own. The photographs show people ready for "selection" and "special handling." They appear stunned, exhausted, confused, yet relieved that their hard journey is over, and that they can at last see sunlight again and breathe the open air. No doubt we arrived in the same condition. We too thought that the worst was over. As our train passed slowly through the camp, we could see people outside, walking around, working, watching from a distance. "There is life here," one of us said. "At least everyone is still alive." This kind of wishful thinking came to an end in the "selections" at the railway ramp.

The ritual of this "selection" process, of course, had a long history before I passed through it. After earlier experiments, the Nazis had smoothed out procedures at the ramp, and by now the SS made their "selections" —

dispatching prisoners to death or to labour —
in assembly-line fashion. Thus, in terms of the
history of Auschwitz as a whole, we Hungarian
Jews came at the end of the line, when the
murderers were in high gear and the whole operation was simply murder incorporated. This
was the Holocaust in final form, mass slaughter
at the end of a history of trial and error. Jews
didn't live long around here. Generally, four
trains from Hungary arrived at the ramp every
day, dumping out a daily total of some 12,000
to 14,000 Jews. Reports indicate that traffic was
heavy, crematoria worked full blast, and warehouses were filled with the belongings of
victims. The camp was so full of corpses that
pits were dug to burn bodies in the open.
Braham estimates that, all told, almost 435,000
Hungarian Jews arrived at Auschwitz in this
summer of 1944, and only about 40,000 came
safely through the "selection" and escaped the
gas. I was one of them. After this, in fact, I
would survive "selection" after "selection" at
Auschwitz, on and on, day in and day out. The
SS search for the failing and "unfit" made "selections" a daily routine in the camp, and every
morning I stood for hours under the eyes of
doctors or nurses of some kind. But the first
"selection" at the railway ramp was the tragedy
of my life.

There, when the doors of our boxcar were

opened, the first men that we saw were dressed in striped prison clothes. These were camp workers, mostly Jews of Polish origin, whose task was to get us out of the train and form us up into lines, separating men and women, along the ramp. Most worked in silence, but some of them whispered a message to us: give the babies and little children to your old people. My mother took Sossy from the arms of my sister Liebe. With this, an SS guard ordered Liebe and me to move away to another group of people lined up for "selection." But Liebe turned back to be with her child. We separated. Quickly my family was gone, lost from sight in the mass of old people and children. I imagined, of course, that they would reappear, that we would see each other again. However, I know now how things worked on the ramp. The young and healthy, those aged somewhere between their teens and up to fifty or so, passed through the "selections"; the others, children, the old, mothers with infants, the sick, these went directly to the gas chambers.

What a terrible thing. When I think of the Holocaust, of what it did to my life, I think most of these moments on the ramp. I have lived them over and over again in my mind. They were the beginning of a sadness in my life that never goes away. I keep seeing Sossy's face. I see Liebe turning back to be with her. I see

My "mother,"
Bodnar Civye.

Chaye Sossy,
Liebe's daughter.

Murdered at Auschwitz, 1944.

My sister Liebe (left), with her husband, Moise Fuchs, and
me at Tasnad. Liebe was murdered at Auschwitz, 1944.

Auschwitz, 1944

Our Rabbi, Maximillian Brisk,
murdered at Auschwitz, 1944.

my family in a crowd of bewildered people about to be murdered together. What a terrible thing was done to us at Auschwitz. What a terrible thing was done to Jewish people. What terrible enemies we have.

Against these enemies, against the shock caused by their power and cruelty, it took time to strengthen one's will to survive. For me, the beginning came in an incident after the "selections," as I was standing with other women who had come through the line with me. Passing by was a girl, a prisoner, carrying a heavy pot of soup for the labour barracks. For some reason, and at risk to herself, the girl turned and walked directly to me. "Cup your hands," she said, and she poured some of the soup into my hands, unwashed and dirty from the long train journey. Nothing had been worse on the train than the suffering from thirst. I arrived weak, dehydrated, and nearly deranged from lack of water. The soup, as little as it was, restored me. With me at the moment was a childhood friend, Cippy Brisk, daughter of one of our Tasnad rabbis. I remember raising my hands to her lips so that she could share the soup. I never saw again the girl who gave me the soup; Cippy was soon separated from me and no doubt ended in the gas chamber. However, the memory of that little moment stayed with me. There was something good about it. The Nazis

Auschwitz, 1944

were trying to reduce us to creatures less than human. Against this, we needed to keep a sense of ourselves as a people worthy of survival. In this sense, surviving did not depend only on getting enough to eat; it had a moral dimension. No matter how much the Nazis tried to degrade me, I tried to hold on to my identity as a moral person.

On the first day in camp, outside our barracks, building C in block 20, we were told to undress. The shame was devastating. As an Orthodox Jewish girl I was never allowed to expose any part of my body, even in a bathing suit, to male eyes. Here male guards were all around us, watching and mocking as SS women shaved our heads and bodies and led us nude to the showers. When we came out, our clothes were gone, and in their place each of us was given an old, dirty dress, always too large or too small. This we wore around the clock, day and night, in bed and out. With this loss of the very clothes I was wearing, nothing remained with me from the world outside. All connections were broken with my previous life in Hungary. Now I was a citizen of Auschwitz and, as a homeless Jew of the Holocaust, this is where my second life began. I came into it naked.

Nakedness, filth, lice, hunger, these were part of the everyday humiliations of life in the camp. They have been described as forms of "useless violence," cruelty with no purpose other than to degrade its victims. Degrading victims was the way of the world at Auschwitz. Primo Levi believes that the SS there needed to see the Jews this way, as a people wretched, dirty, and contemptible. It was good for their conscience to see us as a low and inferior race. "The victim must be degraded," Levi explained, "so that the murderers will be less burdened by guilt."

The memory of the savage and senseless ways in which the SS tried to degrade us came back to me recently when I watched for the first time the famous Holocaust film *Kitty: Return to Auschwitz.* This is the story of Holocaust survivor Kitty Hart, a woman who, by coincidence, was confined to the very same block and barracks in which I lived at Auschwitz. The film is a record of her return visit to the camp in 1978 with her son, to whom she tries to communicate the terrible cruelties which she saw there. Of course, it is difficult for one generation to communicate with another on any subject. About Auschwitz, this communication perhaps is impossible. I understood Kitty, but I could see that her son did not. And being at Auschwitz did not help him. The place was too silent and empty. It was haunting for me to watch Kitty move about through the same rooms where I once walked. But Auschwitz simply was not the same. The rooms were vacant and the landscape had turned soft and green. Grass covered the once-bare ground; weeds covered the railroad tracks. The camp had become a park, a museum. The place I remember in the spring of 1944 was filled to overflowing with useless violence, with suffering, and with Jews, thousands and thousands of Jews. More than Jerusalem, Auschwitz was then the centre of the universe for my people. We were at the heart of darkness, the terrible pillar of smoke and fire described in our holy books. When Kitty went back there in 1978, Auschwitz had become a place for tourists.

When I was there, the Nazis were all business. And business was never better. There were so many prisoners that we lived crowded in upon each other. In the barracks, we craved privacy and space, yet, at the same time, we were anxious to become lost in the crowd. By day, when not on work crews, we sat on our bunks, in silence, head down, fearing to be noticed, singled out, and "selected." At night I slept on a double-sized bunk side by side with six other women, so packed together that when one of us moved, the others had to follow. I still smile when I recall that one of the women in my bunk was the daughter of a famous rabbi from the Hungarian town of Sighet, and so honoured was the rabbi among us that we gave his daughter a certain respect as well. Every night, we waited until she wanted to turn in bed, and we turned with her.

Nights were a time when a process of "natural selection" took over in the barracks. People died at night, the weak and starving. In the morning their bodies were thrown in heaps outside the blocks, so that, for us, each day began with the sight of corpses. New day, new victims. Dead bodies simply went with the landscape at Auschwitz, yet those of us who had lived to see the light of another day in the camp felt a morbid temptation to look at each one of them, searching for faces that we had seen alive the day before. These corpses made bad company. Some prisoners were overcome by this everyday presence of death. You could see it in their faces. The light went out of their eyes and their expressions turned hollow and vacant. But others, living in the same company of death, became more determined to survive.

In the first place, survival meant staying alive. Staying alive meant getting enough food and water. Of these, there was never enough to survive for very long. The daily rations doled out by the Nazis, a slice of bread and a bowl of soup at noon, was the slow road to starvation. So survivors learned to scavenge in the garbage for scraps and peelings. When it came to water, the race went to the swift. Practicing sadists, the guards made a game of our desperate thirsts. They kept us standing *en masse* in front of the door to a room where the water taps were located. Then came a command releasing us to drink. A mad rush headlong for the taps. The strongest ones crowded inside the room, pushing to get at the taps while the weak crowded outside, waiting helplessly — as the guards closed the door. I was always hungry at Auschwitz, always thirsty, but after a while I learned to scavenge with the scavengers and to run with the hounds for water.

Save yourself was the rule. But it was not the only rule. One of the women in my block had arrived pregnant in the camp and passed through the "selections" by concealing her condition. The Nazis had a policy: pregnant women and women with children went straight to the gas. Somehow, month after month, despite daily inspections, the woman kept her secret. So did we. Yet we knew the ending was bound to be tragic: there was no chance for new life in this place. Giving birth meant death for mother and child alike. When the woman began labour, other prisoners gagged her mouth so the guards would not hear her screams. When she gave birth, the baby immediately was strangled and the remains concealed in the garbage. To save a life is a high moral act in Jewish law; to save a life one can violate the Sabbath. The Talmud says, "Who saves one life, it is as though he has saved a whole world." Here, to save one life we had to take another: save the mother, kill the child. Auschwitz was an evil place; nothing good could come out of it. But there was some good in surviving. Later on, it meant so much to me to learn that this women had survived and that she and her husband had a new life together in the United States.

Mostly, survival was a matter of the self. Each of us in the camp worked every day at the individual task of staying alive. Group survival was beyond our means; for this, we had to depend on the powers outside. News of Auschwitz was everywhere by this time. Why did no one come to help us? This is a question that everyone, Jew and gentile, must come to terms with. Every Holocaust memoir asks the same questions: where was God, where was man, where were the nations? I have read since that various Jewish, American, and British figures called on Allied military commanders in the spring and summer of 1944 to bomb Auschwitz, to blow up the death installations and the railway lines. Allied planes, it seems, could reach the camp from bases in Northern Italy. However, Allied military plans gave priority to military and industrial targets, not to Jews awaiting death in camps and ghettos. Thus bombers were sent

Auschwitz, 1944

to strike at the industrial works at Monowitz, a satellite camp just a few kilometres from Auschwitz where prisoners worked as slave labourers in the manufacture of synthetic rubber. Meanwhile, the main death camps at Auschwitz, where the worst crime in history was taking place, remained at peace. In the calm of this little corner of Poland, the SS worked on undisturbed to kill as many Jews as they could before the enemy arrived at the gates.

Some of what they did seemed crazy and incomprehensible, part of the mad, surreal history of the camp. In effect, Auschwitz was both a slaughterhouse and a theatre of the absurd. One bizarre bit of sadism, for example, was the Nazi practice of sending ill prisoners to be cured at the medical infirmary, and then dispatching them straight to the death chambers. Nor was it just a legend that Auschwitz had an orchestra. I saw and heard it with my own eyes and ears. Heavenly music at the gates of hell. The musicians were about six women, prisoners like ourselves, but appearing almost angelic in their clean dresses and long hair. Crowded around them, we must have looked like refugees from the wreck of the world, standing dumb and bewildered, in dirty, ill-fitting clothes, and with hair shaved almost to the skull. The scene was thought-defying: culture and death. This way for the music, that way for the gas.

There are today, of course, some hurtful lies about the good life of music and entertainment at Auschwitz. Some who deny the Holocaust claim that the place was in reality a kind of vacation camp where Jews lived at leisure among parks and swimming pools. This lie began with the Nazis themselves. I remember their giving us postcards to send back home to neighbours in Hungary, assuring everyone there that we were happy and well in our new surroundings. Historians say that these cards — most carrying the simple message, "Arrived safely, I am well" — started arriving in Hungary in the last weeks of June, postmarked from "Waldsee," a fictitious placename concocted by the Nazis to suggest a location of woods and waters. Probably one of these cards was mine. I addressed it to one of my neighbours, but I never learned whether it arrived.

"Waldsee" was pure death in 1944. The pace of destruction caused waiting lines outside the gas chambers and kept the labour crews in the crematoria working in shifts day and night. Bodies were everywhere, and still the "selections" continued and the death lines grew longer. One morning in late summer, standing with other women under the eye of a medical inspector, I sensed that the "selection" had finally caught up with me too. Was this my day?

This time the routine seemed different and the SS nurse kept us standing on the spot. At this point, I had lasted three months at Auschwitz; the thought came to me that I was not going to last one day longer. So I waited for the end in the way so many others had waited before me: naked, head shaved, numb in body and soul.

We waited for hours. Any minute I expected to see the trucks coming to take us to the gas. No trucks came. Finally someone arrived with an order for us: Jews, back to the block. What happened? Probably I will never know. But right after this, things turned around in a hurry. First a surprise: we were given warmer clothes. Next a number of us were marched to the railway ramp. Back onto the trains we went, and back through the gates and out of Auschwitz. Another train ride, but this one took me in a different direction. I did not know it at the time, but the worst was over. Auschwitz was behind me; ahead was slave labour in Germany. The Nazis, desperate to find workers for their factories, had turned to the doomed of the death camps. With the Third Reich dying, the Germans were becoming tangled up in their priorities. The SS was packing into Auschwitz every Jew it could lay its hands on; German industry was taking some of the healthy ones out again to keep the war economy running back home.

So, at death's door, I got a second chance. Historians say that inspectors for the industries of the Third Reich now had their own "selections" at Auschwitz in search of healthy workers. Was this why I stood so long, naked and shaved, under the eyes of medical examiners, awaiting the trucks to the gas chambers that never came? Was I waiting in a death line or a life line? Was I saved by the sheer overload of bodies that tied up the crematoria? Or by Hitler's sudden discovery that he needed Jews in Germany after all? "Germany for the Germans," he always said, "foreigners and Jews out." But at last his racial policies came into conflict with the need of his war industries to get all the labour they could find. Events started to play tricks on Hitler. First he cleaned out the Jews from Germany; now foreign Jews were coming to take their place.

Arbeit macht frei, "work makes you free." This was the lie written on the gates of the concentration camps. For me, however, the lie was true in a way. Work saved my life. Really, to be more accurate, the words on the gate should have been, "Work makes you a slave." But even slaves are worth something when their masters need their labour. The warm clothing handed out to me after my "day" at Auschwitz was a sign that the Nazis at least wanted to keep me alive a while longer. Work made the difference.

Auschwitz, 1944

Primo Levi has described how the nature of work changed in the camp system. At first, when the Nazis had little need for workers, they filled the time of the inmates with senseless and degrading labour. For example, the women at Ravensbruck camp, he reported, were made to shovel piles of sand from place to place, around in a great circle, until the sand came back to where it was lying in the first place. Meaningless work for useless lives. With the new need for labour, however, some of these lives had value again. From a useless piece of flesh I was changed into a useful piece of property. Some writers say that this change was not very great: instead of killing me on the spot, the Nazis now intended to work me to death. Extermination by work merely took the place of extermination by gas. Maybe so. In the meantime, however, I was still alive.

I look back on the train out of Auschwitz as my journey out of the Holocaust. In his documentary film on the Holocaust, *Shoah*, French director Claude Lanzmann returns again and again to footage of trains and railways as if these things were as much a part of the destruction process as the gas chambers. I understand what he means. For Hungarian Jews, death travelled by rail. Many survivors have described the "entry ritual" into Auschwitz, the arrival at the railway ramp, the line-ups, the "selection," the death lines and life lines. In contrast, the exit ritual is less familiar. My memories are of a direct march to the ramp and some minutes of milling around before boarding. The cars were filled with women of many nationalities, though most were survivors of the Hungarian Holocaust. Among them, here and there, were faces from Tasnad, the small remains of a now-vanished community whose women and children had arrived at this same ramp three months earlier.

This time conditions on the train were better — good enough for slaves at any rate. There was air and space, enough water, and even a little food. Not only that, but on this trip the threat of death hung over Jews and Germans alike. By this late date in the war, Allied aircraft were holding open season on anything that moved on the ground in Germany. As a result, our train crawled with caution into this tormented country. At intervals, there was some shunting back and forth in railyards as carloads of prisoners apparently were dropped off at work locations along the way. With them went most of the Tasnad people, so that there were only three of us still together when we reached Salzwedel, the small town about seventy miles southeast of Hamburg where I would work at forced labour for the rest of the war.

Auschwitz, 1944

The Germans had transferred a munitions works to an old building in this out-of-the-way location in order to escape the Allied bombing. After 1945, when Germany was divided by the Cold War, Salzwedel fell just inside the East German boundary, and so, sealed off behind the so-called Iron Curtain, it became unknown territory to western historians. Hopefully, with the new unification of Germany, we soon will know more about this awful place during the Third Reich. The forced labour camp there was one in a string of such camps connected to the large concentration camp at Neuengamme near Hamburg. Across Germany similar camp systems stretched in all directions, giving the Third Reich in its last years a vast camp population of foreign workers. Part of this population was made up of Jewish women like myself, but other types of foreign workers were everywhere in German industry. Large numbers of so-called "volunteer" workers, men for the most part, had been conscripted in occupied countries and transported to assigned camps in Germany as paid labourers with the right to move about in relative freedom. Other workers were prisoners of war, particularly Russians and Poles captured on the eastern front. So, before the Allied armies set foot on German soil, the nation had already been "invaded" by an industrial army of foreign workers.

Just as at Auschwitz I had been part of a mass of people transported to the killing centres from almost every nation in Europe, so at Salzwedel I was part of another international population brought together as a result of the Nazi death business. The idea was maddening — that we were making the weapons that made it possible for the Nazis to kill more people. In my job, I worked at machines that turned out bullet shells by the thousands. At times, in packing bullets into boxes for shipment, I thought about how many more Allied soldiers and civilians, how many more Jews, would be killed by them.

We estimated at the time that there was a foreign labour force of about 10,000 at Salzwedel. It was made up mostly of volunteer workers, particularly from France, together with a good number of prisoners of war, largely Poles and Russians, but including British, French and some Italian soldiers as well. In the women's camp for forced labourers, our number was perhaps five hundred, mostly Hungarian Jews transported with me from Auschwitz. Strict rules segregated these categories of workers. Volunteer labourers were free after work hours. In contrast, we were under the eyes of women guards in SS uniforms, and our life was limited to the factory, the barracks, and the walk in between. Generally the authorities treated volunteer workers as volunteers and Jewish workers as Jews. This meant, for example, that when Allied bombers were over Salzwedel, the volunteer workers were moved into shelters. We Jews, believe it or not, were locked up with the shells and explosives in the ammunition shed.

Still, Salzwedel was not Auschwitz. We slept in single bunks. The meals were thin: coffee and a slice of bread for breakfast, soup and bread for lunch and supper. But the soup at least was thicker, and sometimes there was a slice of salami at the end of the week. Even so, over the winter the rotating twelve-hour work shifts, twelve hours at the machine and twelve in the barracks, over and over, around the clock, wore down my health and strength. Fortunately someone helped me to keep going. Marcel was a young volunteer labourer from France who worked as a mechanic on our machinery. Almost every day he found a way to hide a slice of bread for me somewhere near my machine. Although contact between us was strictly forbidden, we became companions at a distance, without anything more than smiles and glances between us. One day Marcel smuggled a ring to me that he made out of some gunmetal. Stamped on it was the number 1372, my worker identification number at Salzwedel. As far as I know, none of the Hungarian Jews at

Auschwitz in 1944 had numbers tatooed on their arms. The time was too short and too late. My Salzwedel number was the only identification that the Nazis gave me. Probably it was the most that Marcel knew about me at the time. The liberation ended our friendship. But I still keep the ring. It is the one thing from this sad time that brings back a happy memory.

Besides this, nothing at Salzwedel was good to remember, not even the liberation at the end. Emotion swept the labour camps at the first sight of the American 84th Division in the streets of the town on April 14, 1945. But the following events were not so pretty. The Americans gave the town over to crowds of liberated prisoners and labourers in what was described as "a day of free robbery." And rob they did. Homes were invaded; stores were looted. This time it was German citizens who closed their curtains and peeked out in fear at enraged people in the streets. So wild was this liberation carnival that the historian John Toland gave some pages in his book on the end of Nazi Germany, *The Last 100 Days*, to an unsettling description of this crowd gone berserk at Salzwedel. Women pillaged the shops and dressed in the finest they could steal. Drunken men argued and brawled. Nationalities fought nationalities, and gentiles turned on Jews all over again. To end it, Toland remarks, the Americans had to lock up most of the labourers in the camps again.

Thus even the holy rage of Nazi victims could not bring a good end to the war at Salzwedel. I mentioned earlier that the Holocaust survivor Kitty Hart lived in the same block at Auschwitz as myself. She was also at Salzwedel in these days of the liberation riots. In *Return to Auschwitz*, she recalls how she followed the mobs in taking vengeance upon the open town. "I had to follow," she wrote. "For years I had dreamed of the moment when I could at last get my own back." At first I followed as well, but my heart simply was not in it. In fact this frantic celebration of liberation brought on the most black despair. There was no way to get even for what happened; there was no way to get my loved ones back. Now, when the Holocaust was over, I sensed how much I was a victim, and how powerless I was to do anything about it. Something terrible had happened in history, something that could never be undone. Someone said that not even God can change the past. During the "day of free robbery" at Salzwedel, I "robbed" only some old curtains from the factory and some sheets from a bed. And when I finished making myself some new clothes from them, I waited for someone to come to get me out of that place.

I want to conclude my Holocaust story by

describing something that happened to me at Salzwedel. One day, a day when I happened to be in charge of keeping order in the barracks, an SS guard saw smoke coming out of our chimney. Inside, we simply were burning some waste paper. The guard thought we had stolen some coal. He took out his anger on the person in charge. He slapped me across the face so hard that I fell to the floor. Who would not feel rage at this moment? But I want to make a different point: this was the first time that a German laid a hand on me in violence. Holocaust history cannot be told without horror stories, but horror stories are not the worst part of it.

Many witnesses have described Nazi savagery: the SS tortured, maimed, strangled; they shot women and children; they dashed out the brains of babies. These things happened. Probably they have always happened in history; the Huns did them, the Mongols, Crusaders, modern revolutionaries, on and on. Sadistic violence is human enough. It makes lurid history. To me the worst part of the Holocaust was the dull part, the most inhuman part, the step by step "processing" unto death of helpless people like those of my Tasnad community. Maybe I think this way because the Holocaust of us Hungarian Jews probably was the smoothest and most efficient mass slaughter of all. No doubt there was a mad idea behind it, a lunatic anti-Semitism, but what I saw were policemen, railway workers, soldiers, and guards. They roughed us up all right; they made an "example" of anyone who dared to look them in the eye; sometimes they raped and murdered by their own hand; but mostly they seemed to be doing what they were told. They worked us along from place to place, camp to camp, line to line. And they kept the lines moving. When they were finished, most of us were dead.

The whole experience took heart and soul out of me. When Hitler came to power in Germany in 1933, I was a little girl growing up in a little place far away. I never hurt anyone. I loved my home. I wanted so much to feel a part of my country. In 1944 the government of this country took me and members of my family from our home and turned us over to the Nazis. The Nazis murdered my mother and sisters in Poland. They shipped me into Germany. When the war was over, I was homeless. The idea of homelessness is very old in Jewish thought. Orthodox rabbis teach us that Jews in Europe are living in Exile, in the diaspora, and that life for us here away from our Holy Land is wretched, black, the starvation of body and soul. In Germany after the liberation I had a feeling of being in Exile as never before. I was not where I was supposed to be; I was not at home. I remember that General Charles de Gaulle came to Salzwedel after the liberation and told the French labourers there that their motherland awaited their return. I could feel the emotion. I wanted to be part of something again, a family, a people, a nation, a home somewhere. But where was home now?

Auschwitz, 1944

Between Germans and Jews

- three -

The Bible tells the story of a survivor. Noah was a righteous man whom God decided to save from a great flood which was about to eliminate all humankind. Not only was Noah chosen to live himself, he was chosen to save all life on earth, to bring the whole of creation into a new existence after the deluge. After the Holocaust, some Jewish survivors, those most overcome by the Nazi onslaught, found it difficult to recover the spark of life. Others of us sensed that, like Noah, we had a mission to start creation over again. We wanted to locate lost relatives, to marry, to propagate life, to raise families, to affirm ourselves and the existence of our people. I have read that a philosopher said that the Jewish people after the Holocaust have a new commandment: Thou shall grant no posthumous victories to Hitler. Hitler had failed in his purpose to destroy us in his lifetime; now that he was dead we had to bury him once and for all by preserving our Jewishness and multiplying the Jewish presence in the world.

Much has been written about the "mystery" of Jewish survival through the ages. My part in this survival after the Holocaust was no mystery

Bergen-Belsen, 1945-1948

at all to me. After what I had come through, I was not about to play dead for anyone. I remember that I was skin and bone at the time of the liberation, worn down by hunger and hard labour. As a result, the authorities first sent me along with other survivors to a hospital in Hamburg for a period of rest and recovery. There I got a good idea of what the war had done to relations between Germans and Jews. Before our arrival, the hospital had been treating German soldiers and civilians who had been wounded or burned in the war. Abruptly the Allied authorities ordered the German patients out of the hospital and Holocaust survivors into it. German doctors and nurses thus saw their German patients, many with horrible injuries, moved out of their beds and Jews moved into them. I could see the anger in their eyes. But I was in no mood to sympathize. The war was over, yet Germans and Jews were not at peace. Both peoples had just come through the worst catastrophe in their history, and both were determined above all to look first to their own survival.

Someone said a new Jew was born in the death camps, one harder and tougher than before. I guess that Hitler's attempt to put an end to the Jewish people made us even more zealous to go on living as Jews. I was unable in the camps to live the kind of Jewish religious life that I lived before; nevertheless, living in the camps made me want to hold on to my Jewish identity more strongly than ever. This is what the camps did to many of us. One result was that Jewish hearts and minds turned as never before to the idea of Zionism, the idea of a separate Jewish nation in Palestine to preserve the existence of the Jewish people. Everywhere, Zionism now was becoming the great movement for Jewish survival in the post-Holocaust world. After the camps, this was no mystery to me either.

I saw in Zionism at this time a form of vengeance against the Holocaust, a protest against what European civilization had let happen to my people. The particular ideas of this movement, the ideas of Theodor Herzl and the other founding thinkers of Zionism beginning at the end of the last century, were not well known to me at this stage. My Jewishness had always been religious, not nationalist or political. Although there was some talk about Zionism in my family home, the thought of going to live in Palestine was the furthest thing from my mind. To me, home was Transylvania. But the Holocaust changed that forever. I was not going back there, no matter what. The Allies in 1945 wanted to return all the uprooted peoples of the war to their old countries. They called this "repatriation." I was not about to let them repatriate me. In consequence, I became a "stateless person." Worse, I was a stateless person in Germany. In this situation, without family, without home, without roots, desperate for belonging, I was ready to respond for the first time in my life to the idea of a Jewish national homeland in Palestine. But my further education in this idea had to await my next stop in Germany, a place with another dreadful name in history: Bergen-Belsen.

Who has not seen the shocking newsreels of the concentration camp at Bergen-Belsen at the time of the liberation by the British in April 1945? Probably the best known film footage in Holocaust history is the scene of the bulldozer there ploughing piles of corpses into mass graves. History books say that Belsen was not a death camp by design. The place was built late in the war as a detention camp. In the last months, it filled to overflowing when the Nazis used it as a dumping ground for all kinds of prisoners from the eastern camps, which were about to fall into Soviet hands. When food and water ran out, these prisoners dropped like flies. Auschwitz killed by systematic murder; Belsen killed by neglect, by starvation, disease, and exposure. The British buried the remains. By the time I arrived there in the summer, the survivors had been moved into military barracks about a mile from the camp.

There the British were organizing a major camp for the mass of war refugees that everyone began to call "displaced persons" or simply DPs. What a place to try to begin life again after the Holocaust. I wanted to get away from everything that Belsen represented. My first thought there was to get out, and to go someplace else, someplace where Jews were wanted.

That place, Zionist organizers told me at Belsen, was Palestine. I learned in my first weeks there how much they wanted and needed me — and every Holocaust survivor like me — in their struggle for a Jewish homeland. Zionist groups were active everywhere in the camp, organizing life from top to bottom. All activity was Zionist activity. I came to admire, almost to love, the Zionist representatives at Belsen, particularly the instructors who came directly from Palestine, full of idealism and commitment to their cause. They organized classes on Zionism and the Hebrew language. They prepared us to make *aliyah*, that is, the journey to the new homeland in Palestine. These fellow Zionists, I believed, really cared about me, almost in the way of my parents. I wanted so much to join with them, to be part of their adventure.

In my eyes, this Zionist adventure was full of inspiration and poetry. Every Jewish person knows of the ancient Biblical prophecies about the "ingathering of the exiles," the return of our people from the four corners of the earth to our home in the Promised Land. After Auschwitz, it was natural for me to think of Zionism in these religious terms. The whole history of the movement came to seem holy to me. The origins went back to the 1880s when Jews from Russia first settled in Palestine at a time when the area was still part of the old Ottoman Empire. The path was always hard. Zionists had to struggle against a native Arab population for land and survival. They had to struggle as well against British authorities who moved in to control the area after the First World War, and who, in response to Arab demands, tightened restrictions on Jewish immigration into Palestine. Before the Holocaust, Zionism was an uncertain enterprise; after the Holocaust, its message hit home: the Jewish people needed a Jewish nation. After the threat of common destruction in Europe, we grabbed hold of the vision of a common future in Palestine. Overwhelmingly, Zionism seized the imagination of the Jewish people, and the survivors of the camps and ghettos started a great migration to the Holy Land. Such was the success story of Zionism. In my early months at Belsen, I believed that my own life would soon become a part of it.

The Nazis took me out of the quiet life of a

small-town Jewish community in Hungary and threw me into the world events of Jewish history. After Auschwitz, the momentum of these events seemed to be carrying me toward Zionism, *aliyah*, and the mission of pioneering a new Jewish homeland. The journey to Palestine, of course, would be dangerous and illegal, with British authorities in Europe keeping watch at border posts and seaports to hold back Jewish migrants to the land of their ancestors. But I was eager. I was ready to commit myself to all the hard work and sacrifice that I knew awaited me in Palestine. In fact I wanted the hard work and sacrifice; I wanted to give myself to the cause of my people. Frankly, I was never the camping type, but I remember that I wore a knapsack on my back when I slipped out of Belsen to make *aliyah* to Palestine with a group of about two hundred other pioneers. Unfortunately, we did not get very far. Somehow our plan to reach a seaport fell through. When a key contact person on our escape route did not show up at the right time, we were stopped and turned back at the Belgian border. Within days I was back in my little apartment in Belsen again, back in Germany, back to the life of waiting in a DP camp.

This world of the DP camp had an important history of its own. Here was where the Jewish people picked up the pieces. After being nearly destroyed in the Holocaust, we tried in the camps to get our bearings again, to count our losses, locate our missing, reunite our families, and think about starting over. Everyone in Belsen seemed to be looking for someone else. The urge to marry and multiply appeared to be part of survivor psychology. As a result, Belsen turned out brides, grooms and babies by the numbers. Having children, someone said, was a way to take revenge, to replace at least some of the lives which we had lost. Others wanted to get the dead back. Bulletin boards were covered with messages for family and relatives lost in the Holocaust. Camp newspapers carried page after page of notices in search of the vanished. Lists and photos of the missing were everywhere. Most of these lost souls were gone forever. Some came back from the dead. I know this at first hand. One day, out of the blue, there was a knock at my door. It was my brother Bumi.

My baby brother arrived dirty, hungry, and no longer a baby. Like the rest of us, Bumi's life had become a Holocaust story. Working and living by his wits in a labour battalion around Budapest, he had survived the war, the Nazi occupation, and the final slaughter of Jews by the Arrow Cross, the fanatical gang of Hungarian fascists who took over the city in the last days of the war. Arrow Cross jackboots rounded up as many Jewish survivors as they could lay hands on, shot them in batches, and dumped their bodies in the Danube River. After coming through all this, my brother nearly ended up in a Soviet prison camp when Russian troops in the liberation of Budapest mistook him for a Hungarian soldier trying to escape from the city. Returning to Tasnad, where a few Jewish survivors were starting to trickle in, Bumi got news of a near miracle: our brother Moise had survived the labour battalions on the eastern front. The Americans found him after the liberation in Buchenwald concentration camp, a virtual skeleton, crawling on hands and knees, near death from typhus. Fortunately, medical workers were able to nurse him back to health, although Moise was never to be a strong person again. At Tasnad, Bumi heard as well of my own survival. Immediately he set out to find me at Belsen, covering much of the journey on foot.

So, in Germany, house of horrors for Jews, the surviving members of my family came together again. Bumi stayed with me at Belsen and soon we made contact with Moise, who came to live in a DP camp near Munich in the American zone of occupation. Always we hoped that our mother and sister would appear from somewhere. Inside, we knew the truth. This is what made it so hard to be in Germany. The curse of the German DP camps was to live in the nation that had murdered our people. A deep and visible hatred grew between Germans and Jews in these years. At Belsen, recognized as a Jewish camp and run by a committee of our own people, we made rules that forbade Germans even to set foot in the place. Jewish rage was real and raw; I could feel it within myself. Yet more and more Jews, Jews from all over Europe, kept coming to Germany.

Germany had an odd place in Jewish history at this moment. Jews had lived with anti-Semitism in Europe for two thousand years, until the Germans taught us in the Holocaust that we had better not try to live with it any longer. One lesson appeared plain enough: get out of anti-Semitic countries while the getting out was good. Strangely, the despised nation of Germany was the way out. To enter the DP camps there was to escape the old nations of Europe, to become stateless, to come under the protection of the Allies, and to get in line for emigration when the day came to empty out the camps and finally end the Second World War.

For these reasons, Jews kept coming to live in the nation that had just tried to destroy them. Bumi came; Moise came. Others came from Eastern Europe, where anti-Semitism rose up after the war just as dark and ugly as ever. One of them was a handsome young man from Poland. Myer Berkowitz was a tailor who started up a small shop in Belsen together with another man who happened to be engaged to one of my girlfriends. One day this girlfriend introduced me to Myer and said she thought that I would get to like him. Right she was. I married him four months later. Like most women in the steady parade of brides at Belsen, I was married in a borrowed dress that had been passed on from one wedding to another for years.

My husband and I were quite different personalities. He was quiet, serious, withdrawn, a very private person. I was more lively, talkative, easier with other people. What we shared, of course, was the whole style of life and living that came from our Jewish upbringing. Although we came from different countries, we shared as well the same Yiddish mother tongue of most Old World Jews. Significantly, we were alike in another way too — we had both been through the Holocaust. When we married at Belsen on August 20, 1947, I had with me those in my family who survived the Final Solution: Bumi arranged the ceremony and Moise gave me away. Myer had no one. There was no one left. The Holocaust took his whole family. The hurt and loss went deep into his personality. As

Getting married in my borrowed dress at the
Displaced Persons camp at Bergen-Belsen, 1947.

Myer and I, Bergen-Belsen, 1947.

I came to know Myer, I also came to know something about what he went through in Poland. The Holocaust was one, but its history was different from nation to nation and year to year. My story was about Hungary, about Auschwitz, about the end of the Holocaust when the killing was down to an assembly-line process. My husband's story is about Poland, about mass shootings, about the beginning of the Holocaust when killing operations were still raw and primitive. I said that my Holocaust experience could be told without horror stories. His was a horror story from beginning to end.

My husband was born on May 15, 1914, to an Orthodox Jewish family of Novogrudok in White Russia, a mainly Jewish town located about a hundred miles west of Minsk. As a child during the First World War he saw German soldiers for the first time when they occupied this region of old Czarist Russia. These Germans, however, were different from those who came in the Hitler years. In fact the Jews looked upon the Germans of the First World War as a people less anti-Semitic than their own neighbours and more tolerant than Russian Czarism. How different were the Nazis who came to Novogrudok in 1939 when the area was part of eastern Poland.

Hitler must have done something terrible to the mind and spirit of his people. The Germans were ferocious in Poland, savage and cruel to the Poles and savage and cruel beyond comprehension to the Jews. Hitler hated all Jews, and Polish Jews most of all. In his book, *Mein Kampf*, Hitler describes his shock and disgust when, as a young man in Vienna, he first saw Jews recently arrived from eastern Europe with their black clothing and traditional beards. He came to hate the foreign, Yiddish-speaking world from which they came, the world of the *shtetl*, the small, rural towns where the great mass of East European Jews lived and flourished. Woe to this world when Hitler came to power in Germany.

Jews had lived in Novogrudok since the fifteenth century. The town was within the so-called Pale of Settlement, the large area of western Russia where Jews were contained and controlled in Czarist days in a kind of vast rural ghetto. Those who believe that Jews are rich need to know about life in the Pale. This was a world of Jewish poverty, where life was hard and hand-to-mouth. In one of the great emigration movements in modern history, many Jews left the Pale in the 1880s, moving to the New World in search of a better life. The rest stayed and endured in the teeth of the worst anti-Semitism in Europe. Here, strangely enough, in the hardest circumstances, Jewish culture in the West found its richest expression, in art, literature, music, drama, folk culture, in ideas and political movements of all kinds. Here was the centre of Jewish civilization in Europe. Poland, with over three million Jews after the First World War, was the heart of it all. Quite plainly, this is why Hitler wanted to destroy it. To the Nazis this was the reservoir of European Jewry, the biological source of the Jewish people. Thus Jewish Poland had to be annihilated. Novogrudok went with it.

Just as my brother Bumi wrote a history to remember the Jews of Tasnad, so Holocaust survivors from Novogrudok have written a memorial book about their lost community as well. The work describes over four hundred years of Jewish life in the town. Novogrudok was a *shtetl* in traditional style, with the Jews living clustered together in town and the Poles scattered about on small farms on the outskirts. Jews ran the shops in the main section (on so-called Jews Street); they worked all the trades, crafts, and services; they carried out almost all the public functions. Even the whole fire department was Jewish. By the 1930s, out of a population of around 32,000, over 18,000 were Jewish. This majority was enough to give Jews control of all the seats on the town council, although, by rule, the mayor had to be a gentile. The inner life of the Jewish community itself remained the business of the *Kehilla*, the traditional council of local Jewish dignitaries, which served as a form of Jewish self-government within gentile society. Here at Novogrudok was the Jewish world of eastern Europe through and through. Where Tasnad had two synagogues, Novogrudok had as many as fifteen. To look at the old photographs in the memorial book of the town is to see a Jewish community filled to overflowing with life and energy. Page after page of group photos show religious organizations, study circles, tradesmen fraternities, and political groups from left-wing to right-wing. In the hard soil of Poland, Jewishness at Novogrudok flourished and branched out in all directions.

This is the way that Myer remembers his

town, full of Jewish life and colour. But trying to make a living there was a different story. The economy of the *shtetl* was strictly bare-bones, with too many people chasing after too little work. Myer's father had to hold down three trades at the same time to make ends meet; he worked at once as a shoemaker, a glazier of windows, and a hauler of lumber. To help out, Myer's mother sold milk from the family cow. For the children of this working family, there was not much more than the prospect of entering trades already overcrowded with workers. Both of Myer's brothers became barbers and his sister took up work as a seamstress. Myer himself left school after his Bar Mitzvah at age 13 and began a long apprenticeship to become a tailor. Unfortunately, however, Novogrudok was full of Jewish tailors, and in 1933 Myer decided to try his luck at the trade in the nearby city of Vilna (now the Lithuanian capital of Vilnius), which was then part of Poland.

If anything, Vilna was more Jewish than any other centre in the region. It was said that at Vilna even the stones spoke Yiddish. The place, Myer told me, had over six hundred Jewish tailors in these years. Still he was fortunate enough to be hired into one of the better shops, a business employing no less than ten other tailors. There he stayed until 1939, when events closed in on the Jews of Poland. Myer saw trouble coming. Seated at his sewing machine one day in 1939, he heard a noisy commotion in the street outside. Vilna was in the middle of a pogrom. Mobs were breaking into Jewish shops, beating up the Jews inside, and tossing them out windows onto the street. Pogroms against Jews, of course, were nothing new in Poland, but this one was a sign that anti-Semitism was reaching a high pitch in the country even before the Nazis arrived. But with the coming of war in September, 1939, the Jews faced a level of violence that left all pogroms far behind. Polish anti-Semitism was bad enough, but no one saw anything like what Hitler was going to do.

The outbreak of the war brought Myer back to Novogrudok to be with his family. His younger brother, Welvel, who had been away in the Polish Army, returned home as well after Germany and the Soviet Union made short work of the Polish forces. Hitler and Stalin, of course, had agreed early in 1939 to divide Poland between them, and as a result all of eastern Poland came under Soviet control. So the Russians got to occupy Novogrudok first. They turned the place upside down in no time. Stalin was then full flush in his five year plans to collectivize the Soviet economy, and he immediately set out to do the same thing in Poland. Polish farmers at Novogrudok were dragged kicking and screaming into collective agriculture. Jewish businesses were national-ized, and some of the more wealthy owners were denounced as "bourgeois capitalists" and sent off to Siberia (a stroke of fortune for some, as it turned out, since they were not around for the Holocaust later on). Remark-ably, Myer's own house was taken over by the state. His father, to increase his small income, had always rented a few rooms in the back. Lo and behold, this made the house a "capitalist enterprise," subject to seizure by the govern-ment. In general, the Russians simply kicked around anyone who got in their way at Novogrudok. But at least they just wanted to control and communize the place. Rumours and refugees coming over from Nazi-occupied Poland carried stories of far worse things: star-vation, atrocities, and ghettoes. When Hitler turned on the Soviet Union in June, 1941, the Nazis brought this way of life to Novogrudok as well.

Many writers describe the fury of the Nazi onslaught that began Operation Barbarossa, Hitler's holy war against the Soviet Union. Ger-man soldiers, filled with years of Nazi racism and hate propaganda against Soviet "Judeo-bolshevism," seemed to want to smash Russia to pieces and grind the Jews into dust. As the *Wehrmacht* tore through eastern Poland, German planes used firebombs to level Novogrudok and every *shtetl* in the region, reducing everything to wrack and ruin. The Nazi occupation of the town — or what was left of it — was mean and murderous from the start, with beatings, shootings, and hangings beginning in the first days. The first shock at the outset was the mass shooting right in the centre of town of about a hundred Jewish men picked at random on the street. But the really large killing operations were still to come. These were the work of the *Einsatzgruppen*, the SS mobile killing squads that roamed from town to town, carrying out the systematic mass shootings of Jews that marked the first stage of the Final Solution. The Novogrudok region was the killing field of so-called *Einsatzgruppe B*, death units operating behind the lines of German Army Group Centre. On the days when *Einsatzgruppe B* came to town, the world stood still in Novogrudok.

Throughout the whole period of the war, though, the everyday terror in town came not from Germans but from Latvians, Lithuanians, Estonians, Ukrainians, and White Russians. The German occupation unleashed all the Jew-hating gangs in eastern Europe. With a green light from the Nazis, they came miles to do their dirty work on the Jews: beating, robbing, blackmailing, killing. Novogrudok, of course, had its own anti-Semitic brutes who joined in this racking of helpless victims. One of them once beat Myer so badly with a wooden board that he was barely able to walk. All of these groups were the bloodhounds of the Nazi occupation, tracking down Jews who failed to wear the yellow star, who tried to hide, to escape into the woods, or to disguise themselves as gentiles. As plain, Jew-hating fanatics, they were worse than the Nazis. But they were not as genocidal. When it came to killing the Jews of Novogrudok, men, women, and children, no one did it like the *Einsatzgruppen*.

The Hungarian Holocaust that I saw was done with trains and gas chambers. Myer saw the Holocaust at a rough and ready stage, when the killing was done by military methods, with firing squads mowing down victims in batches and burying them in mass graves. According to most testimony, the *Einsatzgruppen*, after rounding up their victims, generally took them by truck or on foot to a remote location some distance away where the killing could be done out of sight and sound of the population. At Novogrudok, they did not bother with this. Units of *Einsatzgruppe B* made four trips to the town between 1941 and 1943. Each time, they took their victims only a short distance away, killing them within easy earshot, and burying them in mass graves at the four corners of the town.

Bergen-Belsen, 1945-1948

These murderers were busy in smaller settlements around Novogrudok before they arrived there for the first time in December, 1941. Their appearance marked the beginning of the "ghettoization" of the Jewish population. With a lot a shouting and shoving, the Germans ordered the Jews out of their homes on the cold day of December 5 and drove them toward the bombed-out shell of the town courthouse. This building was to become the so-called working ghetto, the place where the Nazis confined skilled workers and anyone else who might be of use to them. The rest of the Jewish people were crowded into a second, makeshift ghetto located a few streets away. First, however, the *Einsatz* killers took their toll, beginning their slaughter in the town with the most helpless and "useless" part of the population: old people and children. Myer remembers that it was a rainy day when a large number of them, perhaps several thousand, were massacred on December 8 near the edge of town. Among them were his mother and father. The shooting was loud and clear to every ear. The mass grave was in plain sight.

For almost a year after that, Myer lived in the working ghetto. He feared that tailors in the ghetto would be sitting ducks for Jew killers, and so he told the Germans that he was a glazier, because in the past he had sometimes worked with his father at repairing broken windows. For this reason, he was given a pass that allowed him to work at jobs outside the ghetto in the daytime. Bombing raids in the war had left Novogrudok with plenty of broken glass to repair, and Myer discovered that the way to survive was to keep working, stay out of the ghetto as much as possible, and disappear whenever the Nazis were looking for Jews for one reason or another. Whatever the reason happened to be, the frequent result was that the Jews ended up dead. So Myer stayed alive by staying invisible. After watching his disappearing act time after time, his companions in the ghetto began to call him "the ghost." In August, 1942, he survived the second sweep of the *Einsatz* units: another massacre, another mass grave. The Jews of Novogrudok were being wiped out, lot by lot, and the survivors in the ghettoes were counting the days until the killers came back again. Some Jews didn't wait around. On a day in November, when the White Russian guards at the ghetto were in a drunken stupor, Myer fled with others into the woods. There, in the cold winter, near starvation, sick with scurvy, his clothes crawling with lice, his body covered with boils, Myer was near despair.

He had lost his mother and father to the *Einsatzgruppen*. His younger brother was killed by the Germans in the battles at the time of the

Soviet retreat from Poland. His older brother, Moise, had been murdered in a tragic scene. Moise had lived with his wife and child in the nearby town of Baranovichi. When *Einsatz* soldiers swept this town, his wife and child were shot and killed. Sometime after, Moise's nerves broke under the strain. "Murderer, murderer," he screamed at a Nazi on the street. The Nazi took him aside and shot him. Now, of Myer's family, only his sister, Rachel, remained alive, locked up in the working ghetto with her husband and child of fourteen months. Desperate to save her, Myer returned to the ghetto. He slipped through the gates by mixing quietly with a group of Jews who were sent out each day from the ghetto to carry back water from a well in the area. His plan was to slip back out with his sister in the same way. But his plan did not work. Helpless, Myer and Rachel waited with the dwindling number of survivors in the ghetto. Both lived through the third round of *Einsatz* killings on February 4, 1943. The Nazis always played a sadistic game on the day after these massacres. Normally the food ration in the ghetto was barely enough to keep a body alive. After the shootings, the Germans "celebrated" the occasion by increasing the ration for the day. Following this third slaughter, there were not many left to feed, and not many left to shoot. On May 7, 1943, in the final mas-

The young Myer (left), his sister Rachel (center) and
brother Welvel (standing), with friends.

sacre of the Jews of Novogrudok, *Einsatzgruppe
B* killed Rachel and her baby.

Myer told me a story about a dear little Jewish boy around eight years old whose luck at
surviving the killings was the talk of the town.
Time after time the Nazis led him away to be
shot; time after time he came back alive. The
Cat, they called him — the boy seemed to have
nine lives. Sadly, nine lives were not always
enough for Jews in eastern Europe. The Cat
was murdered by *Einsatz* platoons on the
fourth and last sweep through town. To me,
this story has a point: Myer must have been
very lucky. Any Jew in Novogrudok who survived longer than the Cat had to be very lucky.
In fact, there were only about one hundred

and twenty of them left in the ghetto after the fourth *Einsatz* massacre. One thing was clear: they would be the next and last in line. The Nazis simply had no other Jews to kill. Secretly, this surviving remnant started to dig a tunnel out of the ghetto. The work took almost six months. Men dug in the passageway most of the night and piled the dirt out of sight in every hiding place they could find. On September 24, 1943, the last survivors of the Novogrudok ghetto crawled out of the tunnel into a rainy, pitch black night. Some were shot in flight and others were recaptured close by. Myer was with the few who escaped into the woods.

There, over the winter of 1943-44, he lived in a camp of armed partisans in heavy forests to the east of Novogrudok near Minsk. Fighting a twilight war behind German lines, this band of about 1500 Jewish men and women survived on the dwindling supply of food that could be forced out of Polish farmers. Most of these farmers already had been pillaged and picked clean by other raiding parties, Germans and partisans alike. The earth was bare and the people on it downright savage. Even in the woods, Jews had to keep an eye over their shoulders. Some Polish resistance groups were infected with anti-Semitism, and their members hunted Jews with the same ferocity as they hunted Nazis. Worse still, some handed over Jews to the Nazis. The ghettoes were sure death. But Jewish life in the wild also could be nasty, brutish, and short.

In July, 1944, when the area was liberated by Soviet forces, Myer was down to a primitive state: barefoot, his clothes in rags, his body skin and bones. Still, there was a war on. The Soviets drafted him on the spot into military service and sent him off with the Third White Russian Army as it advanced into the heart of Germany. The fighting was ferocious, a blood-bath for Russian and German soldiers. What saved Myer from the slaughter this time was something simple: he was a tailor. And the Red Army needed tailors. Thus, as Soviet forces fought their way into Berlin, Myer was put to work behind the lines, sewing and repairing uniforms, safe from the killing — for once in his life.

He had come through a lot in the Holo-caust, and he did not want to go through any more. After the German defeat in 1945, as Myer travelled by train back toward Novogrudok, he found himself face to face again with the same old Polish anti-Semitism, this time made more deadly by the fact that some of the worst Jew-haters were carrying guns picked up during the war. Everywhere on his route he saw them hunting Jews again —

on the trains, in stations, in cities along the way. In Bialystok, they came right into a synagogue. Myer had enough. Even before reaching Novogrudok, he turned back and headed for the DP camps in Germany.

At this time, Zionist groups were active in eastern Europe directing Holocaust survivors westward along refugee routes leading to the DP camps and to ships bound secretly for Palestine. The more the camps and ships filled with refugees, the Zionists reasoned, the more western governments would be pressed to open Palestine to Jewish emigration. Myer followed one of these refugee routes, but the Holocaust left him without heart for more hard dangers in Palestine. He remembered that his mother used to write to relatives in the United States, and his hope was to make contact with them again and somehow, when the time came, to get away to a normal life in the New World. He was too hurt inside for anything else. I saw this hurt when I met him in Belsen. I knew that my future with Myer would not be in Palestine But I knew also that he would never get away from the Holocaust no matter where he lived.

Such is the story of my husband's survival during the Holocaust years. I believe that Myer and I could tell most of the history of the Holocaust out of the experiences of our own lives.

We believed, when it was over, that Germany should be made to answer for what was done to us, our families, and our people. Surely such monstrous crimes cried out for justice. We knew, of course, that it was wrong to blame all Germans for what happened. More than any other people, Jews know the evils that can come from ideas of collective guilt. No other people has suffered more from myths of collective guilt than Jews themselves. For centuries we have been accused as a whole people of crucifying Jesus, of scheming against Christianity, of hatching wicked plots and world conspiracies. So we could not believe that all Germans were involved in the crimes of the Holocaust, but we believed that all who were involved in these crimes should be brought to trial.

We deserved to have their guilt made clear to the world. The trials of Nazi leaders at Nuremberg were not enough. There was too much to account for. Out of pure racism and hatred, cities had been destroyed, nations had been plundered, and peoples had been slaughtered. Some of us believed at first that world anger against this outrage would see that the day of justice would come. Now not the Jews but the "master race" of Germans appeared to be the pariahs, the outcasts of civilized humanity. As a sign of Allied wrath, American Commanding General Dwight Eisenhower ordered his troops in occupied Germany not to fraternize with the German people in any way. However, the day of justice did not come. What came instead was the Cold War. Winston Churchill said in 1946 that an "Iron Curtain" had descended across Europe. It came down as well on our hope that the world would do something about the Holocaust. As the Soviet Union more and more was perceived as the danger to western democracies, these nations increasingly looked to the Germans as their allies against "communist totalitarianism."

In this way, German allies became more important to the West than Jewish survivors. And the Holocaust was left to the history books. Anger in the democracies against Germany could pass easily enough once the Soviet Union became the main danger to "the free world." But anger in the DP camps was too deep. No one here was ready to forgive and forget, even though everyone else was moving on. As the United States came closer to the new West German government, the DPs were caught in between, and the continued existence of the camps became an obstacle to further Western unity in the Cold War.

By this time, these camps were communities in themselves. Most had their own schools, newspapers, theatres, and social services. I myself worked for a time at Belsen with a group caring for about seven or eight Jewish orphans who lost their parents in the Holocaust. In doing such things, the camps were a constant reminder of the human tragedy of the Nazi years. Unfortunately, nations wanted less and less to be reminded of this tragedy. The Germans wanted the DP camps to close. So did Western governments. So did the DPs. Everyone wanted the DPs to leave, but no one wanted to provide a place for them to go. On one hand, nations urged the British to open Palestine to Jewish immigration; on the other, these same nations kept their own doors closed. Finally, around 1947, the picture was clear: if the world was going to get the DPs off its conscience, these doors had to open. Not coincidentally, a strong post-war economic recovery in western countries created a new need for immigrant labour. So the old quota restrictions on Jews began to loosen, and the DPs at last moved out of the camps.

Some time before this, Myer had located an aunt in the United States through notices placed in a New York Jewish newspaper. Her letter of reply was not encouraging. The chances for Jews to enter America were still too limited. But through her he made contact with Harry and Nathan Velensky in Fredericton, New Brunswick, who set about against the odds to help him immigrate to Canada. Small

Caring for Holocaust orphans at Belsen, 1947.

chance. At this period, Canada was notorious as a country with practically all doors and windows shut to Jewish immigrants. The sad story behind this has been told in the popular book *None is Too Many* by Canadian historians Irving Abella and Harold Troper. They describe how government officials used tough immigration regulations to keep the country closed to Jewish refugees trying to flee Hitler and the Holocaust in Europe. The result was that Canada, of all democratic countries, had the worst record for admitting Jewish immigrants during the Nazi years.

Some things change, though, and in 1948 Canada's immigration policies changed a lot. The nation announced two new plans for entry: a so-called bulk labour plan, in which workers with essential skills were accepted in large lots (happily, tailors were included in one lot), and a close relatives plan, which provided for applicants with family already living in Canada. After years of getting nowhere with immigration officials, Myer suddenly became easily eligible under both plans. Canada was opening up to Jews again. Remarkably, the country with the worst record for accepting Jewish immigrants soon enough became the country with one of the best records for accepting Jews from the DP camps. For us, an added surprise came on the very day that we were to leave Belsen. Word came that the United States now was prepared to accept us as well. Myer, with bags all packed, decided to take no more chances. That day, March 15, 1948, we left for Canada.

Only recently, a friend of mine found in her attic an old copy of *The Canadian Jewish Chronicle* for October 1, 1948. I noticed on one page a little photograph of a group of immigrants standing in line at the office of the Immigration Department in Halifax, Nova Scotia. Two faces, distant and somewhat lost in the crowd, nevertheless were familiar. They were mine and Myer's. Certainly our arrival in Canada was small news in the large events that the *Chronicle* was describing to its readers in that year. The newspaper was joyous about the bright new day in Canadian immigration policy. "If the present rate of Jewish immigration into Canada continues for the rest of the year," it reported, "1948 will have the largest Jewish immigration into Canada since the beginning of the First World War." However, the grand event for the Jewish people in that year, it continued, was something more joyous still: the founding of the state of Israel. With this, the long Exile was over. At last the Jewish people could be at home in a Jewish nation. The *Chronicle* noted that Jews everywhere were about to celebrate *Rosh Hashanah*, the coming of the Jewish New

Standing in line at the Immigration Department, Halifax, 1948. Myer and I are in the line of people against the wall.

Year 5708, a date marking the beginning of "a wholly new era in Jewish history." After the Holocaust, the surviving remnant of my people, like Noah, was starting all over again.

Reading this news from over forty years ago made me think about my own place in all that happened. The newspaper said that a wholly new era of Jewish history was beginning. But I was not finished with the old era. I never will be. I am a Jewish woman of the Holocaust. That event defined my personality and my outlook upon the world. I was still a young woman when the good ship *Aquitainia* brought me across the Atlantic to live in Canada. Most of my years were still ahead of me — my married life with Myer, my children, my own home. Still, I believe that the real story of my life is about Tasnad, Auschwitz, and Bergen-Belsen. I loved my new country, but I could not stop thinking about these old places.

Remembering

- four -

I am not homeless any more. Five years after landing in Canada, on September 18, 1953, I became a citizen of my new country. As I stood with others in the citizenship court, the judge told us to remember our old homelands in our hearts, but to be good citizens of Canada. To be honest, I felt nothing in my heart for my old homeland. Not after what had happened to me and my family. But I wanted a new country to take its place. I thought at that moment of the final days at Salzwedel when General de Gaulle came to speak to the French workers in the labour camp. He told them that their mother country was waiting to take back her children. This is what I wanted, a country that wanted all of her citizens, even the Jewish ones. I wanted a country that would let me be just as much a part of it as any other citizen. And that is exactly what the citizenship judge, Bacon Dixon, told us. "Now," he explained, "you have all the rights and privileges of a born Canadian." These words and this whole ceremony of citizenship meant so much to me. I later told the clerk of the court, after whom we had repeated the Oath of Allegiance, that one day I would write a book and put his name in it. His name is George Noble.

My home in Fredericton, the small capital city of the province of New Brunswick, is a long way from where I started in Tasnad. Still, when I look at my new town, I think of my old one. Many things about the two places are the same: the same landscape of hills and trees, the same pretty streets, the same small-town atmosphere. In a way, I am back where I started, back in a quiet home on a quiet street in a quiet country. But everything is different. Tasnad and Fredericton are in different worlds. One of these worlds, the old world of central and east European Jewry, is gone with the wind.

Jewish Tasnad vanished in 1944 along with the other small-town communities of Hungarian Jews. According to reports from recent visitors to Transylvania, hundreds of old synagogues in the region still sit abandoned; others have been turned into warehouses, concert halls and other modern facilities. Old Jewish cemeteries are overgrown with weeds and bushes. A rabbi there said that it is best to let the weeds grow. To call attention to Jewish graves when anti-Semites are around, he warned, is to expose them to desecration. I still hold dear the little pieces of earth in Tasnad where my father and mother lie in their graves. But nothing else there belongs to me anymore.

My brother Bumi visiting our father's grave
at Tasnad.

Fredericton

A young friend at my mother's grave
at Tasnad.

My old Tasnad home with my sister-in-law
Ada Fuchs (right) and its present occupant.

When Bumi returned to the town after the war
he found our house occupied by another family and all of our furniture and possessions
long gone and forgotten. In any case, the
whole area now is a part of Romania again. To
punish Hungary for her alliance with Nazi Germany, the western allies returned Transylvania
to Romanian control after the Second World
War. The result, of course, was to rekindle all
the old hatreds between Hungarians and Romanians that I lived with in my youth. So, half a
century after the Holocaust, many things
about the place are the same, except that the
old Jews are missing.

They are missing as well from Myer's old
town of Novogrudok. The place where my hus-

band grew up is now inside the Republic of Belarus. Stalin took it away from Poland when he pushed the Russian border further west at the end of the war. By this time, Jewish Novogrudok was no more. In 1963 there were only eighty Jews living there, most of them new-comers from other regions. The synagogues were vacant. Large government stores had re-placed the little shops of the old *shtetl*, and Jews Street had been turned into a row of apartment houses. Crumbling gravestones re-mained in the old Jewish cemetery, but new roads and construction were closing in on the site. In the four corners of the town, where the remains of victims of the *Einsatzgruppen* lie in mass graves, no marker or memorial has been raised in their memory. Like so many other *shtetls* in the old Pale of Settlement, Jewish Novogrudok died with its people in the Holocaust.

Thus the world of our childhood is dead. Hopelessly, Myer and I keep trying to bring it back to life. A few years ago, we went to Ottawa to be present at the "Canadian Gathering of Jewish Holocaust Survivors and Their Chil-dren," a meeting of people like ourselves from across the country. The year was 1985, a date chosen to mark the fortieth anniversary of our liberation from the concentration camps. Every day we were there, both of us kept look-ing for a familiar face in the crowd, hoping to find someone we had lost, someone who knew about our loved ones, someone to bring back old memories of the world in which we grew up. There was no one.

In a way, I wanted our children, our daughter Sybil and our son Joel, to know and remember this old world of their ancestors. Especially I wanted them to know the beautiful Jewish life that I lived in my father's house. But I could not bring myself to tell them about the ugly things. They were too young and innocent. I wanted my children to have all the happiness of youth, to love life, to feel safe and proud in their Jewishness. All the insane hatred for our people, all the gassing and murder of our families and relatives — I did not want them to know about this. To spare them, Myer and I told them little more than that we were Holocaust survivors. To spare us, they did not ask many questions.

Now they have grown up and moved away to Toronto to a life of their own. They grew up as Jewish Canadians, living in an open society so different from the closed and cramped old communities of our people in central and eastern Europe. Sybil graduated from McGill University and works now as a speech therapist. Joel was trained as an optometrist at Waterloo University and has a practice of his own. I cannot forget what happened to me in far away

Fredericton

Sybil Faith Berk, MA   Joel Boris Berk, OD

Europe. But why should my children remember?

What good are memories anyway? Why dig up the past for new generations to agonize over? Why make Jewish youth bitter about what other people did to their parents and relatives? I believe that some things must be remembered. But I know that others are best forgotten. I think that I understand the temptation to forget the Holocaust. The argument is easy enough to make. The Holocaust happened over forty-five years ago. The survivors are fewer and fewer and soon they will be gone. Most of the murderers are dead and gone already. Those still at large are old men weak in mind and body. When Canadian authorities deported a Nazi war criminal to Germany some years ago, they had to carry him on the airplane on a stretcher. More recently, another accused man appeared in court looking deranged and bewildered, with failing vision and wearing a hearing aid in each ear. Is it time to let bygones be bygones? What good does it do to know about the Holocaust? Some writers say that to know about it is to prevent other holocausts in the future. Everyone knows the saying, "Those who do not know the past are doomed to repeat it." But I am not sure that this is true. Others, in fact, say the opposite: to know about the Holocaust, to know the precedent has been set, is to make other holocausts more likely. Maybe those who know the past are able to repeat it more easily. So what good are memories? The six million are dead; why not let the memory die with them?

There are, of course, some people who want to write them out of history altogether. Sad to say, we in New Brunswick have our own Holocaust denier. Since the actual Holocaust never happened, he claims, there is nothing to remember or forget. Thus Jews have no cause to sorrow over the dead and gentiles have no reason to try to come to terms with what happened. This is the big lie. Such men re-write history because the truth is too terrible for them to admit. No one dares to defend the Holocaust. Knowing how great was the crime of Auschwitz, these men have no way but to deny it. Against their denial of history, our best defense is knowing history and remembering it. To me, denying the Holocaust is worse than forgetting it or not knowing about it in the first place. But sometimes the result can be the same. I think that those who do not know about it, who forget it, or who confuse it with other events in history, sometimes deny the Holocaust in a different way.

One example of this was the verdict in the trial in 1990 of a man named Imre Finta before the Supreme Court of Ontario in Toronto. Finta, a Hungarian immigrant to Canada, was the first person to be tried under new legislation in 1987 which permitted authorities to bring charges in Canadian courts for war crimes and crimes against humanity committed in other countries. During the Second World War, Finta was a captain in the Royal Hungarian Gendarmerie, those policemen in black uniforms and odd feather-plumed hats whom I described earlier. According to the charges, he had been involved in June 1944 in forcibly loading 8617 Jews from a brickyard concentration camp onto railway boxcars in Szeged, Hungary. Witnesses described the brickyard as a place of mud and misery where Jews slept on the ground, used ditches as latrines, and were stripped of valuables before being packed like sardines into the trains. Some of these trains were bound for a labour camp in Austria; others went directly to Auschwitz. Reportedly, a number of Jews died en route. For his part in all this, Finta, who was said to have been in command of the Gendarmerie detachment involved in this deportation, was charged with illegal confinement, kidnapping, robbery and manslaughter. Reading about this trial, I thought of another brickyard full of mud and misery, another deportation, another detachment of Hungarian Gendarmerie. That is, I thought of Szilagy Centre. What had happened to me and my family there in 1944 apparently was happening in the same way and at the same time to Jews in brickyards and railway sidings everywhere in small-town Hungary. What Finta was accused of doing at Szeged other policemen had done to me at Szilagy Centre. I knew I would never see these other policemen on trial, but the Finta case at least was as close as I could come. To me, it was as if they were in the dock with Finta. I thought that some justice at last would be done to these policemen of the Hungarian Holocaust.

Imre Finta was found not guilty. His lawyer argued that the new legislation on accused war criminals in Canada was an attack on "a lot of tired old men who are too weak and sick to defend themselves." What Finta had done in loading Jews on trains bound for concentration camps in 1944, he insisted, was no more than what the Royal Canadian Mounted Police had done in loading Japanese Canadians on trains to concentration camps on the west coast in 1942. True, this defense lawyer admitted, conditions in the brickyard and on the trains were "not pleasant," but they were not life threatening. And if a few Jews died on the journey, the responsibility lay, not with Finta, but with those operating the trains. Nor could Finta be blamed for what happened when these trains arrived at their destination in another country. Granted, Finta did confiscate Jewish valuables, but this, the defense explained, was what his government ordered him to do. This government, said the lawyer, was indeed anti-Semitic; Finta simply had the "misfortune" to live and serve under it. Thus the government alone, and not Finta as an individual, should be held responsible for the things that happened to the Jews in Hungary in 1944. Such were the arguments that convinced a Canadian jury to acquit this old police officer at Szeged. Sadly, I assume that the gendarmes at Szilagy Centre would have received the same verdict.

Writers, of course, have long lamented the failure of nations to do anything about the Holocaust. They say that nothing was done about it when it happened and not much has been done about it since. In Canada, the Finta jury did nothing about it either. In his testimony to these jurors, the historian Randolph Braham urged them not to confuse the Holocaust with other histories. It was not accurate, he insisted, to draw a parallel between what Imre Finta did to the Jews in Hungary and what the RCMP did to Japanese Canadians at the same period. These Jews would gladly have traded places with the Japanese Canadians. If they had, Braham explained, the Jews would have travelled in second class coaches rather than boxcars; they would not have been murdered at the end of the line, and their families would still be together when the war was over. These differences were plain enough to this man who had studied them for most of his life; to the jury, however, perhaps it was less clear how Finta's individual guilt for what happened in the brickyard was connected to the larger guilt for what happened at Auschwitz. I hope that the jury verdict will not be the last word of Canadians on the Final Solution in Hungary. To do better, younger generations will need more light and more knowledge.

I know the Holocaust in a way that these young people never will. The madness that came out of Germany came right to my door, right into my life. Mercifully, it did not last long. Only a year passed from the day in April 1944 when I wore the yellow star for the first time to the day in April 1945 when the Americans liberated Salzwedel. But the memory of that year has taken up the rest of my life. It changed my whole world. And it changed me. When I was young in Tasnad I accepted anti-Semitism as a fact of life: I lived with it, I expected it, I said nothing about it, and I did nothing about it. I am not like that anymore. As old as I am, I will not live at peace with anti-Semitism again. When the British historian and Holocaust denier David Irving came to speak in Fredericton, I got a picket sign and walked in a protest demonstration outside the place where he was speaking. So, I know that memory can make a difference. But it is easy for me to remember the Holocaust; it touched my life. Young people have nothing to remember about the Holocaust from their own lives. They must be told.

Telling may not be enough. Stories of mass death are nothing new in our century. In school, Canadian youth have been told year after year to remember and honour the dead of the world wars. Yet when Remembrance Day comes each year on November 11, it is mostly old people who turn out to the ceremonies; the young just take the day off from school. I want the Holocaust to mean more than simply

My brother Moise and his family in Israel.

another day to remember the dead — or to forget them. I know that it cannot live on the memories of older generations alone. To be remembered, the Holocaust must mean something that the young want to remember for their own good, something worth holding on to for their own experiences to come. I remember the Holocaust for the sake of the past. They must want to remember for the sake of the future.

I see hope for this. Something unusual is happening. Most events make the news for a while and then fade from memory. Strangely, the Holocaust made little news for about a generation after it happened, but then it began to take hold of the public imagination. Apparently more and more people recognized that something terrible and important had happened to the Jews during the Second World War and they wanted to know and hear more about it. Today, this interest is still growing. There is more talk than ever about the Holocaust, more television, more films, more books. No matter how much the Holocaust deniers tell their lies, more people seem to want to know and remember what really happened.

Things are happening in government as well. To make up for the shame of the closed-door policies of the Holocaust years, Parliament has opened the country to more refugees and immigrants. When Myer and I first came to Fredericton in 1948, it was a city of English and Scots, British subjects still close to the habits and loyalties of the old country, and to people of their own kind. Now we see faces and hear names from every part of the world. There are now new laws against hate mongers in our country. For over forty years, numbers of alleged war criminals lived freely in our midst, but now we have laws to try to bring them to trial in Canadian courts. So, after a long delay, our government at least is starting to catch up with the Holocaust.

But new laws are not enough. The response to the Holocaust cannot come from above,

Myself at Bergen-Belsen, 1947.

from Parliament and the courts. It must come up from below, from the citizens of the country. Especially it must come from the new generations. Older people have always taught the young about the world through stories. I hope that my Holocaust story will help them to know and remember more about the experience of the European Jews of my time. I survived the Holocaust. Now I want the memory of the Holocaust to survive me.